TRUTHS AMONG US

Conversations on
Building a New Culture

Interviews by
Derrick Jensen

PM

ALSO BY DERRICK JENSEN

TRUTHS AMONG US

Conversations on
Building a New Culture

Interviews by
Derrick Jensen

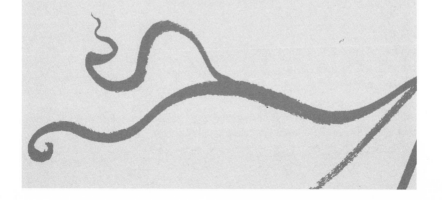

The following interviews appeared in slightly different form in *The Sun*: George Gerbner, Luis Rodriguez, Judith Herman, Marc Ian Barasch, Paul Stamets, and Martín Prechtel.

Truths Among Us
© Derrick Jensen 2011

This edition © PM Press 2011
All rights reserved.

Back cover photograph by Derrick Jensen
Cover and interior design by Stephanie McMillan
Edited by Theresa Noll

10 9 8 7 6 5 4 3 2 1

ISBN 978-1-60486-299-7
LCCN 2011927943

PM Press
PO Box 23912
Oakland, CA 94623
www.pmpress.org

Printed in the USA on recycled paper, by the
Employee Owners of Thomson-Shore in Dexter, Michigan.
www.thomsonshore.com

CONTENTS

INTRODUCTION

George Orwell wrote that in times of universal deceit, telling the truth is a revolutionary act. In that and many other senses, the people interviewed in this book are revolutionaries. In these interviews and in their other work, they individually and collectively peel back layer after layer of the lies that are this culture—to reveal some of the foundational lies essential to and inherent in capitalism, conquest, land theft, genocide, ecocide, racism, sexism, rape culture, and so on.

George Gerbner describes some of the ways that television socializes men to be men and women to be women—that is, within a patriarchal society, teaches men to be dominant and women to be submissive—and how TV socializes us all to be fearful. Stanley Aronowitz details some of the parallels between science and fundamentalist religions, and lays bare the desire for control—and the fear of death—that underlies so much of science. Richard Drinnon talks about the inherent relationship between racism and empire-building. Judith Herman discusses the effects of trauma and captivity, including domestic violence, on our psyches and our social relations. Jane Caputi explores the personal, political and mythological ramifications of living in a rape culture, and what we can do about it.

A doctor friend of mine often says that the first stop toward cure is proper diagnosis. This is as true of social ills as it is for medical ones. The authors interviewed in this book provide that first step—diagnosis—and also lead us to action.

Another way to say this is that in order for us to act, we must first perceive the atrocities, and to do that we must peel back this culture's lies that mask the atrocities. These authors do that, and point to ways we can join them in active opposition to this culture.

GEORGE GERBNER

Interview conducted at the
Fort Mason Center in
San Francisco, January 20, 1998.

George Gerbner fought fascism for a long time. Born in Hungary, he emigrated to the United States in the 1930s to get away from the Fascists, then returned to Europe during World War II to fight against them. A member of the U.S. Army, he parachuted behind German lines and fought alongside the partisans.

Through much of the twentieth century he fought another sort of fascism, the totalitarianism of corporate conglomerates that effectively govern our country and control our media. He no longer parachuted behind enemy lines. He counted murders and analyzed the stories told on television.

By the time children turn eighteen they have witnessed more than forty thousand murders and two hundred thousand other violent acts on television. They have also seen approximately four hundred thousand advertisements, each delivering essentially the same message: Buy now and you will feel better.

What are the effects of taking in this volume of violence? How do advertisements affect our perception of the world? George Gerbner's analysis moves far beyond facile descriptions of violence begetting violence. The effects are far more subtle and insidious, and they are infinitely more dangerous.

Gerbner was a founder of the Cultural Indicators Project, an organization formed to study the relationship between violence in the media and society at large, and the Cultural Environment Movement, an umbrella of organizations dedicated to democratizing the media. He edited nine books, including *Invisible Crises: What Conglomerate Media Control Means for America and the World; Triumph of the Image: The Media's War in the Persian Gulf, An International Perspective;* and *The Information Gap: How Computers and Other Communication*

Technologies Affect the Distribution of Power. He wrote extensively on the relationship between human behavior and the stories that help to form us.

I met George Gerbner in San Francisco on January 20, 1998, while he was on a whirlwind speaking tour. We talked in the corner of a small cafeteria, focusing on the question Gerbner studied for decades: what does it mean to each of us when corporations tell all the stories?

George Gerbner: A few centuries ago, the Scottish patriot Andrew Fletcher wrote, "If I were permitted to write all the ballads, I need not care who makes the laws of the nation." He was right. Ballads, or more broadly stories, socialize us into our roles as men and women and affect our identities. Our parents, schools, communities, churches, nations, and others used to be our society's storytellers, but over the past fifty years this role has been taken over by marketing conglomerates and people who have a great deal to sell. This transformation has profoundly changed the way our children are socialized. It has made a significant contribution to the way our societies are governed. It has changed the way we live.

In the average American household the television is on for seven hours and forty-one minutes per day. That's a lot of time, but that's not the main problem. The main problem is that the stories we see and hear on TV are very limited, despite the deceptive proliferation of cable channels. Shows may vary in style or even plot, but the elements I consider to be the building blocks of storytelling, casting and fate, are strikingly similar across the board. Think about the characters that animate the world of prime-time drama, which is where most of the action and most of the viewing time is. What is their demography? What is the fate of the different groups—men and women, young and old, rich and poor, and so on? The studies I have conducted with the Cultural Indicators Project show that character casting and fate follows stable patterns over time.

Derrick Jensen: What types of patterns?

GG: Men outnumber women in prime-time television two to one, children, elderly people, and nonwhite people are underrepresented, and poor people are virtually absent.

DJ: Please explain why this is important.

GG: Socialization—the telling of all the stories—is what makes us develop into who we are; stories teach us our social roles. People who are well-represented in stories see many opportunities, many choices. The opposite is true for those who are underrepresented, or are represented only in a particular way. For example, women between the ages of twenty-five and thirty-five are generally cast only for romantic roles. What message does that impart to young girls growing up? We have a contract with the Screen Actors Guild to study why so many of its female members stop getting calls when they're thirty-five, and only start getting them again when they're old enough to play grandmothers. What does that invisibility teach women about their roles in society? Men play romantic leads until they totter into their graves. How does that affect people's perception of their opportunities for love, sex, and human companionship?

Casting dictates the demography of the symbolic world. Think about the ratios of success to failure and victimizer to victimized experienced by various demographic groups in the world of television. If you look at who is consistently doing what to whom, you see a great homogeneity. It's a strictly regulated and relatively inflexible system.

The over- or underrepresentation of demographic groups in these stories leads to a skewing of the types of stories that can be told. Because most scripts are written by and for men, they project a world in which men rule, and in which men play most of the roles. Scripts are constructed to satisfy the demands of a market—which is not, by the way, the same as the demands of an audience. Because a film or television producer cannot really hope to make money solely in the United States, most producers target their stories for a world market. What themes need no translation? What themes are essentially image-driven, universal? Sex and violence. The demands of an international market reinforce the predilections of male writers.

And society's patriarchal power structure ensures that men are the ones having sex and wielding weapons onscreen. Year by year, you might see a 5–15 percent change, but never a steady trend toward greater diversity.

DJ: How do you know all this?

GG: The Cultural Indicators Project is a nonprofit formed to study not only violence on television, but the relationship between the stories we are told and society at large. Every year we take a sample of characters in prime-time dramatic programming and add them to our database, which by now contains profiles of some forty-five thousand characters. We've been doing this for thirty years, during which time the patterns have been stable.

DJ: I'm still fuzzy on how "casting and fate" affects the real world.

GG: How does schooling affect the real world? By socializing us. Casting and fate work the same way, except the lessons they teach us start in infancy and continue throughout life. Television has become the universal curriculum.

Television and movies project the power structure of our society, and by projecting it, perpetuate it, make it seem normal, make it seem the only thing to do, to talk about, to think about. Once viewers have become habituated to a certain type of story, they experience great consternation if you try to change it. Let's say you try to countercast, or change the typical casting in a typical story. Now a woman wields power. She uses violence. Suddenly, the story gets wrapped up in describing why this is so. It has to revolve around why a woman is doing things that seem scandalous for her, yet normal for a man. Telling a story different from what the audience has come to expect disturbs public sensibilities.

DJ: So in a sense television is representative of the culture.

GG: It is representative of the power structure, not the culture. This means those in power are overrepresented, they're more likely to be successful, and they're more likely to inflict violence than to suffer it.

DJ: Okay. So it's not really representative of the power structure, but instead the fantasies of those in power.

GG: Exactly. It is an agency of the power structure by which those in power represent their fantasies. By doing so they contribute to those fantasies becoming real, becoming a part of the consciousness of each of us.

When it comes to creating stories it is the supply that determines the demand, never the other way around. Just imagine a group of writers talking about ideas, and someone says, "Why is it that most of the time the victim is a woman? Why don't we equalize the scales?" The answer would be, "A violent woman is distasteful."

DJ: But it's not distasteful for us to see Bruce Willis blow away hundreds of people.

GG: To me it is distasteful, but it is also expected.

DJ: What does taking this volume of violence into our bodies do to us? We did not evolve perceiving unreal images. A hundred years ago if you saw someone get slashed with a knife you were probably quite traumatized, because you were witnessing someone's actual injury.

GG: Most of the violence we see depicted is pretty sanitized. It has none of the tragedy, none of the gore. Certainly not on television. Much of it is what I call "happy violence," that is, cool, painless, and spectacular. It's designed not to upset you or gross you out, but to entertain you and deliver you to the next commercial in the mood to buy. I think people are still shocked when they see violence in real life. We have anecdotal evidence of children, when they see somebody actually getting hurt, saying, "That's not like in the movies."

I don't believe that the frequency or explicitness of violence are the primary issues. Violence is a demonstration of power, and the real issue, once again, is who is doing what to whom. If time and again you hear and see stories in which people like you—white males in the prime of life—are more likely to prevail in a conflict situation, you become more aggressive. If you are a member of a group or a gender that is more likely to be victimized in these stories, you grow up more insecure, more dependent, more afraid of getting into a conflict, because you feel your calculus of risk is higher.

That is the way we train minorities. People aren't born a minority, they are trained to act like a minority through cultural conditioning. Women, who are a numerical majority of humankind, are trained to act like a minority. The sense of potential victimization and vulnerability is the key.

Of course not all people react the same way to stories. Women of color may react differently to their sense of potential victimization than men of color. We have to ask, again, how have they been socialized to behave? Who takes what role? What power relationship is being demonstrated? Most of the time people talk about violence as if it were a simple act. But it is a complicated scenario, a social relationship between violators and victims.

For every ten violent characters there are about ten victims. For every ten women who are written into scripts to express the kind of power that white males express with relative impunity there are nineteen women who become victimized. For every ten women of color who are written into scripts to act in an aggressive way, there are twenty-two women of color who are victimized. Your chances of victimization double if you are not a member of the group for whom it is accepted to be a victimizer, who are more likely to be aggressors and less likely to be victims.

DJ: But doesn't that just represent reality? Although in domestic violence women sometimes beat men, it is overwhelmingly the other way.

GG: Children are not born into these roles. Stories teach them how to act, whether they are to act the victim or victimizer, how and toward whom they may or may not express their aggression. Both men and women learn that women are legitimate victims, receptacles for aggression. White males are not acceptable victims. Having shaped reality, these stories then reflect it.

It takes a conscious decision to not conform to the roles assigned to us within these stories. Even our decision to rebel is based on what we have seen; rebellion depends on having something to rebel against, and that, too, is provided in the culture, in the stories.

DJ: Don't these stories then not only determine who does what to whom but also what we see as acceptable modes of conflict resolution? Instead of two people hashing out their differences, we see them fight it out.

GG: Yes, because creating lively and realistic dramatic intercourse takes talent. Most violence on TV betrays a poverty of imagination. It's an easy way out on the part of writers and producers who want to create the cheapest, most easily exported product.

Violence is not even what audiences want. It depresses ratings in every country. But because violence is a universally understood theme, it is still profitable. Even though it's not what audiences want, they have become accustomed to it.

Over time the violence has grown more extreme. In order to stand out in a market already saturated with violence, it is necessary to outdo the others. This is especially true in movies. There used to be about 20 million people going to movies every year. Now, many times that number watch television each night. This means producers of mainstream movies have had to ask themselves what it is that viewers don't get enough of. These producers must not only appeal to expectations emplaced by television, they have to go beyond what television can offer. Extreme violence falls into this category.

The limitations on violence in TV shows are not put into place out of a sense of morality, but because producers know that advertisers don't want to be associated with excessive violence. The message that advertisers send to stations is straightforward: "Deliver the audience to my commercial in a mood to buy. Whatever else you do, that is your job." So in a strange way, advertisers act as a moderating force on the worst of the violence.

DJ: The moderation of advertisers is at best a double-edged sword, though, since it also pretty much guarantees you won't see television programs attacking the corporate structure.

GG: Absolutely. TV producers don't want to bite the hand that feeds them. And it's ironic, because television is broadcast in the public domain. The airwaves are public, not private property. But in the United States, Americans are never told the airwaves belong to them. They think the airwaves belong to the networks.

DJ: CBS isn't going to tell them any differently.

GG: Of course not. Ask yourself, why is there essentially no political diversity in the United States? It's because there's no choice of ideologies on television. You have a single party, consisting of two factions: the Ins and the Outs. When the Outs get in, they do the same thing as the Ins were just doing. You cannot have a democratic government if there are no strong ideological differentiations, which means that you've got to have a capitalist party, a socialist party, greens, indigenous groups, anarchists, a communist party, a fascist party, and so on, each of which should command significant airtime. In all other "democratic" countries that is what the media laws try to do.

It is the First Amendment in the United States Constitution—which states that government shall make no laws abridging freedom of the press—that forbids government from diversifying what goes on the air. The first amendment was designed to assure that the expression of diverse opinions was not prohibited by the government. But the framers of the constitution didn't anticipate precisely what has happened, which is that this country is run by a private, nondemocratic government of, by, and for corporations. This has led to a situation in which a handful of conglomerate directors, maybe five or six men, and they are almost always men, determine the stories that socialize our children.

DJ: And the underlying motive of these directors is to accumulate ever-more power and money.

GG: Power and money. They go hand in hand. They are indivisible.

DJ: But it's not a conspiracy. A friend of mine once told me, "You don't have to have a conspiracy when everyone thinks the same."

GG: A conspiracy is a plot that fails. Conspiracies never succeed. They may make little ripples in the power structure, but that's all. What we're talking about here is the system. People act similarly, not even necessarily because they want to, but because there are rules, and there are penalties, and because if you don't play by the rules someone else will.

DJ: Let's go back to violence for a moment. Do media depictions of violence lead to more violence in real life?

GG: Not particularly. A Cultural Indicators Project comparison of heavy and light viewers, controlling for all other factors, showed that people who watch more television are not particularly more aggressive. People know that violence in everyday life is stupid, it doesn't work, and you get hurt, so most avoid it.

However, there is no way to avoid fear. The overall message of television is one of victimization and insecurity, so the major effects of exposure to TV violence are dependence, emotional vulnerability, and in fact a lack of aggressiveness. It would be much better if people were more aggressive. Perhaps then they would begin to stand up for their rights. People are taught to be too submissive, they are taught to be insecure. They are taught to be afraid.

DJ: But I've heard a hundred times that TV violence leads to violence.

GG: From what source did you hear this? The notion that exposure to violence incites violence is itself media-driven. When I go on talk shows, the producers never let me talk about anything else. They ask, "Does violence on TV incite violence?" I say, "No," and they say, "Thank you very much, and now a word from our sponsor." They never let me get to the next sentence, which is, "Television does something much worse than incite violence. It cultivates a sense of insecurity and dependence that makes people submit to indignities no human being should ever have to submit to."

DJ: I take it from all this that you are not against all depictions of violence.

GG: Oh, no. Violence is a legitimate dramatic and artistic feature, and it is necessary to show its tragic effects and consequences. But these consequences are hardly ever seen; sponsors don't like it.

Also, violence is necessary, and has historically been necessary, when people have had to strike out against unbearable odds. When people are given no other avenue of opposition or revolt, they have only violence, and they must use it.

DJ: That's another reason real depictions of necessary violence can't be allowed on the media. With corporations having a lock on everything, they have to keep a lid on the unhappiness they cause.

GG: The notion that media violence begets violence is silly on many counts. Those in power are not foolish enough to incite violence against their own rule. They know very well that television cultivates passivity, a sense of withdrawal and insecurity. That's exactly what the corporate structure needs and wants.

DJ: Let's go back to what you said a moment ago, about violence being shown without its consequences. That should come as no surprise, because our entire culture is predicated on ignoring the consequences of our actions, whether they are environmental consequences, the consequences of smoking, or what have you.

GG: Exactly. This is all so tragic. We happen to have a grant from the Robert Wood Johnson Foundation for a special study of alcohol and tobacco in the media. We found that there are 2.1 alcohol drinking incidents per hour in prime time. TV is saturated with alcohol. In recent years Seagram and others have colonized the industry. Seagram bought MCA, and the rate of drinking incidents increased. These companies are buying up studios to make sure they can control the stories. The consequences of alcohol use are of course rarely shown on TV.

Tobacco use is down on television, with one tragic exception. Young women are smoking more than before, and the fact that we have a tobacco-related lung cancer epidemic among young women is no coincidence. Young women seem to follow the model that television gives them: they assert their independence and rebel by smoking.

DJ: The notion of rebelling by smoking is once again a cooptation of very real feelings of powerlessness that people have, and a desire to rebel against the power structure.

GG: Exactly.

While smoking has gone down on television, it is rampant in movies. It's difficult today to see a movie in which the star doesn't light up in the first scene, and then for the whole rest of the movie smoking is used as a dramatic device, for transitions, for relaxation.

This is criminal, and it's tragic. In order to amass wealth those in power are leading people to use an addictive drug that is guaranteed to kill if used as directed. This is a drug that kills over a thousand people per day, more than all illegal drugs combined. There's never been anything like it, and it is promoted, and legally advertised, and legally sold, and more to the point of this conversation, it is consistently embedded in the stories that socialize us.

DJ: Let's go back to the relationship between media and the corporate state. You've written, "We are headed in the direction of an upsurge in neofascism in a very entertaining and a very amusing disguise."

GG: Fascism is essentially a corporate-run, highly repressive ideology which abolishes political choice and imposes a certain type of ethnic dominance and preference, and it no longer requires a brutal administration and a brutal takeover of culture. It can be accomplished in a very entertaining and "democratic" way. Of course it is far from democratic.

In the last twenty years, the monopolization of our culture has proceeded in a way and at a rate that would have been unimaginable and unacceptable at a time when antitrust was still alive. But there is no more administration of antitrust, and the Telecommunications Bill of 1996, which was passed without any public discussion, opens the floodgates to even further monopolization of our culture. All of our stories are told by a handful of conglomerates. If you count Sony, Time-Warner, Disney, and Rupert Murdoch, what else is there? What kind of a democracy is that?

DJ: It seems pretty clear to me that the reason that fascism can be of the friendly sort is that we go along with it.

GG: I'm not sure I understand the point you're making.

DJ: Indonesia, Guatemala, Chile, the Black Panthers. Those who do oppose are eliminated.

GG: Of course. It's ruthless. Absolutely. We need only think about the Vietnam War. Forty-five thousand American troops were sent to die in a battlefield tens of thousands of miles away. Our neocolonial administration defoliated Vietnam, Laos, and Cambodia, poured dioxin over the people, killed more than a million human beings, and bombed the region back, as they said, into the Middle Ages. Why is it not fascism when it is done a few thousand miles away? Does it have to be here? If you accept what they do elsewhere, they don't need to do it here.

That is essentially what fascism and the stories that teach us how to be social beings have done: make people accept unspeakable brutality, make people accept genocide. We have accepted it, and we have supported it. It continues to this day.

DJ: A lot of what we've been talking about is the monopolization of perception. Judith Herman, an expert on psychological trauma and the effects of captivity, pointed out that one of the central tools used by perpetrators to break the wills of their victims—and this is true whether we are talking about domestic violence or political terror—is to cut off all other social contacts, to monopolize the perception of the victim. It strikes me that much the same thing is going on socially. The reason this is important is that in order for people to remain in captivity, they must believe there are no alternatives. If you can open the victims out, they can think, "Why the hell am I putting up with this?"

GG: I don't think it is sufficient to leave it at that. It is a monopolization not only of perception but of conception. Perception has to do with the senses, but what we're talking about here is the monopolization of one's entire world view, which goes far beyond perception. The stories we tell about the world erect the world in which we live. If you can monopolize the telling of stories, you're going to monopolize perception, you're going to monopolize conception, and you're going to monopolize behavior.

DJ: What is the role of the U.S. media in promoting state violence? I'm thinking of the way the Persian Gulf was handled.

GG: Public consciousness is militarized, by which I mean the public is brought to accept, and even call for, military solutions—which are forms of organized violence—to social and national or international problems.

I call it *Persian Gulf War: The Movie*. Even the name is fraudulent. There was no war. A war is something where people shoot back. Nobody was shooting back. It was slaughter. U.S. planes were strafing columns of fleeing civilians. But very seldom did you see images of any of this. If we would have seen what happened on the ground, a wave of revulsion would have swept over us.

In this context, it's interesting to note that for most of the Vietnam War, we learned about body counts every day, but there were no pictures. The minute they started to show pictures of the war on the ground, those of us who opposed the war knew it was over. That was the end. Showing American casualties was a way of preparing the public to accept a lost war. Until the war is lost, you never show any casualties, except for the enemy.

DJ: The media not only report but influence history. You've called this "instant history."

GG: Instant history is a very interesting new phenomenon made possible by the ability to broadcast an event while it's going on. Those who control the media have the capacity to select the shots, angles, scenes in such a way that the very transmission of an ongoing event helps determine its outcome. This has never before been possible. Even in Vietnam the pictures had to be flown back, which meant at least a six or eight hour delay. By the time you saw pictures of the battle, it may very well have been over. Now, as in the Gulf War, it is possible to broadcast an event while it is going on, and by selecting the images or the shots or the scenes, or editing it in a certain way, you will influence the outcome. All of the major heads of state involved in the Gulf War had the capacity to tune in to CNN and see what was happening on the battlefield—or, more precisely, what they thought was happening. In fact, what they witnessed were selected shots calculated to have certain results.

DJ: Calculated by whom?

GG: The army. Every photographer had to get permission, and they had to follow a guide who told them what they could shoot and how they could shoot it. After that the photos were submitted to army censorship.

DJ: That makes me think about Nestor Makhno. He was a Ukrainian anarchist who first fought against the invading Germans in World War I, and then he fought against the Whites, then the Reds, then the Whites, and then again the Reds. He was so popular among the people that the Reds shot on the spot any of his troops they captured, out of fear his troops would infect their own with a love of freedom. Makhno, on the other hand, gave nonofficer prisoners he captured the immediate choice of joining his troops or going home. Entire combat units of both Reds and Whites defected to his side. He believed deeply in the freedom of the press, and insisted that enemy newspapers in the towns he captured not close down as long as they didn't report his troop movements or, because of endemic antisemitism in the Ukraine, attempt to instigate pogroms.

GG: That is interesting. I know that in several Scandinavian countries, the government subsidizes opposition newspapers, because it's important to have a diversity of choices. In France, there is a 3 percent tax on videotape that contributes to a fund subsidizing independent productions.

But here, production and distribution are monopolized. Ten or fifteen years ago there was a so-called divorcement by the Supreme Court that said that studios that control production cannot control distribution, but that's been forgotten. The Reagan/deregulation era left a long-lasting imprint on our cultural life. Under current political circumstances there is virtually no opposition to the monopolization of culture, in great measure because politicians are so dependent on the media that they cannot raise any of these issues. We have nothing to fall back on except our own citizen movements and organizations like the Cultural Environment Movement.

DJ: What is that?

GG: It is a coalition of some 150 groups in about fifty countries that works for gender equity and genuine diversity of ownership, employment, and representation in the media. We had a founding convention two years ago. Our goal is to democratize the media.

DJ: How do you see that happening?

GG: That's a good question. I wish we had some kind of formula. It's a people's movement. We have no funding. We have tried to raise money through mailings and by applying for grants. We have tried to lift ourselves up by our own bootstraps, which is the only way a citizen can do something without corporate sponsorship.

We have struggled, but we believe in the notion of citizenship, in the possibility of organizing to make a difference. Our motto is, "Don't agonize. Organize." That was an old union slogan in the 1930s. They showed it can be done, and we want to show that it can be done now.

The problem may not be so difficult as it seems. People are ready, and they're searching for an answer. Through this conversation we've talked about the passivity of people, but underneath that passivity there is resentment, even rage. There is a sense of frustration. That has to be tapped and channeled in a constructive way.

DJ: I work a lot with indigenous peoples, and they talk often about decolonizing their own minds. Perhaps one of the first steps in that process can be to redefine ourselves once again as human beings, not as consumers.

GG: Absolutely. Decolonizing is an excellent expression, not only for indigenous peoples, but for all of us. We have to try to do that. People, once again, are ready, and they are creating their own movements.

When I introduce the Cultural Environment Movement at conferences, people often say, "I've been concerned about these issues, but I never knew there was anything I could do." This statement—that people feel helpless about a major cultural issue—is about as powerful an indictment as anyone could ask for concerning the state of our democracy. If people feel helpless, what's the point of pretending?

DJ: In a tangible sense, what do you hope that readers of this interview will do?

GG: This may surprise you, but if I could ask only one thing, it would be that readers demand that producers cast more women, and more women of color. If we can achieve that, the world will begin to change. We will see a more accurate representation of humanity, and we will see a greater diversity of roles. Stories will change. They will not just reinforce the power structure. That simple act— changing our stories—will change future socialization.

DJ: How did you get started studying this?

GG: After the assassinations of Martin Luther King and Bobby Kennedy, the National Institute of Health set up the so-called Eisenhower Commission to study violence. They wanted to scapegoat television, and so we received a grant to study it. I said, "We'll study violence, but in a broad context. We'll study the world violence represents, and the role television plays in it." They said, "Okay, you study that for yourself. We just want to know the violence count." We gave them their count, but more importantly we began the broad study of the cultural environment, the annual monitoring of dramatic prime-time television. We also began studying Saturday morning cartoons, which are even more violent. In prime time the rate for incidents of violence is five per hour, while in cartoons it is between twenty and twenty-five per hour. It is sugarcoated with humor, to be sure, but that makes the pill—the scenario of violence—easier to swallow, to integrate at an even earlier age.

When we were given this grant, I discovered that no one else was studying this. That in itself is another indictment of the corruptness of our system.

Something as fundamental as a study of the stories that shape our lives should be taken up by the Library of Congress or some other major national institution. That can never happen, because Congress will not appropriate money for it so long as it is dependent on the media. Because no one else was doing it, I and a few like-minded people formed an educational nonprofit organization.

DJ: I would like to finish by asking you again about something you've written: "The facts of violence are both celebrated and concealed in the cult of violence that surrounds us. There has never been a culture as filled with images of violence as ours is now. We are awash in a tide of violent representations. There is no escape from the massive invasion of colorful mayhem into the houses and cultural lives of ever-larger areas of the world." When and how do you think this will all end?

GG: We may not succeed tomorrow, and we may not succeed in a lifetime, but the time must come when the dysfunction in this culture becomes intolerable enough to a sufficient number of people to take political expression, and therefore to democratize cultural production and conception. Only then will when we find our way to a more humane and healthy culture.

The goal is not to rid our stories of violence. The goal is diversity, the implementation of a relatively democratic playing field in the area of cultural production. Other countries have gone much further in that direction than we have, and we cannot call ourselves a democracy until we try, too.

STANLEY ARONOWITZ

Interview conducted at his
office in New York,
September 10, 1999.

Stanley Aronowitz has spent his life defending democracy, justice, and the earth. He started his activism as a labor organizer at lunch counter sit-ins, and went on to help plan the March on Washington for Jobs and Freedom in 1962 and 1963. He hasn't stopped since. His activities have included: founding an experimental high school in East Harlem; developing a college program for working adults at the City University of New York (CUNY); and running for governor of New York on a radical democratic program that combined opposition to corporate power with a commitment to sustainability, racial equality, feminism, gay liberation, and individual freedom.

Aronowitz has also authored or edited twenty-five books, including *Against Schooling: For an Education that Matters* (2008) and *Left Turn: Forging a New Political Future* (2006). He has published more than two hundred articles and reviews in publications such as the *Harvard Educational Review, Social Policy*, the *Nation*, and the *American Journal of Sociology*. He teaches at the Graduate Center at CUNY, where he is distinguished professor of sociology and urban education.

His intellectual pursuits are both broad and deep, including labor issues, social movements, science and technology, education, social theory, and cultural studies.

On science, he argues that it has no monopoly on truth, and that no knowledge can be independent of the social context and political hegemonies that created it. Science, despite its claims to objective truth, is in fact an ideology, and one that is based on domination of the living world. This domination is intimately connected to the destruction of democracy. As he articulates so clearly, "The scientific community wants us to have faith in them that they will do whatever is right for us. But I don't believe them. I don't have that faith in anybody, except people collectively deciding what they want to do within their own lives."

Derrick Jensen: You've written, "The power of science consists, in the first place, in its conflation of knowledge and truth." What does this mean?

Stanley Aronowitz: Science is founded on the idea that the knowledge we may gain using its specific mathematical and experimental methods is equivalent to what we mean by truth. The mythology holds that science describes physical reality, that science is truth. And if science is truth, instead of merely one form of truth, then all other forms of truth—all philosophical truth, all ethical truth, all emotional, spiritual, relational, experiential truths—are devalued. They are regarded as something else besides truth.

A lot of this stems from the writings of Immanuel Kant. He helped to separate the discussion of truth from anything having to do with speculation, anything having to do with ethical understanding, anything having to do with art. Scientists may agree that there is something called artistic truth, but they— and I'm talking not so much about specific scientists (although this is often true) as I am about what the scientific worldview does to all of us—don't think artistic truth has anything to do with the material reality that the scientist investigates.

Science is based on exclusion. And not just the exclusion of all these other forms of knowledge. It's full of exclusions. Logic, for example. In order to establish its authority it excludes what might be described as a critical logical analysis that derives not strictly from experiment, but from the more or less informal observations of philosophers, political theorists, and social theorists. Scientists will say, "That's all very interesting, but it's really got nothing to do with truth. It's just your opinion."

If you can convince people that science has a monopoly on truth, you may be able to get them to believe that the knowledge generated through science is independent of politics, history, social influences, cultural bias, and so on. But science isn't independent of these things. What we perceive as a scientific truth today may very well be considered nonsense in a few years. It's absolutely absurd to believe that any paradigm of scientific knowledge is equivalent to the way the world really is (of course you can't say this to scientists, or they go crazy).

Think of some of the changes science has gone through. What was taken by scientists as truth in the era of Aristotle, a period of well over a thousand years, was grounded not only in experiment and observation, but also in a methodological set of assumptions that everybody accepted. Then along came the Copernican revolution, disproving many of the "truths" of this era, and now scientists have a new set of assumptions. What we so firmly believed before is now considered superstition.

DJ: My first degree was in physics, and I can imagine how my teachers would have responded to what you just said. They would have said, "One of the great things about science is how open it is to these revolutions of thought. That is precisely why scientific knowledge is truth, because it allows for evolution, it mutates as we make methodological or experimental discoveries that invalidate our old hypotheses and generate new ones."

SA: I agree with your teachers insofar as a strength of science is its ability to endure and grow from evolutions in thought and methodology. But I have a problem with their belief that every day and in every way science is coming closer to the truth. A fundamental precept of science is that at some point we're finally going to get to the bottom of things. We're going to understand the fundamental building blocks of matter, we're going to unify electromagnetism with gravity, and like Einstein believed, we're going to have a general theory. This conceit is scientists' version of utopian hope. It motivates many to undertake the day-to-day drudgery connected to scientific work.

I'm skeptical about the possibility that we'll figure everything out. There are scientists who take the same position I do, that there will always be uncertainty, there will always be tentativeness, there will always be upheaval. But the majority of scientists believe we are moving toward some ultimate theory. This latter group subscribes to science as a religion.

DJ: What's wrong with that?

SA: First, their religion masquerades as something that it is not. Scientists consider themselves skeptics, and are often highly scornful of people who rely on "mere faith." But science is coercive in the same way that dogmatic belief in a deity can be coercive. Just as God is taken as an axiom by true believers, so the four elements of scientific discourse cannot be questioned.

DJ: Four elements?

SA: The first is the exclusion of the qualitative in favor of the quantitative. If you cannot assign a number to something, it doesn't exist. The second is that except at the outset, speculation is excluded in favor of observation and experimentation. The third is that knowledge is claimed to be free of value. There's nothing inherently wrong in knowing how to make a neutron bomb, for example. It's simply information, so the mythology goes. And the fourth is that method is given primacy in the confirmation of knowledge.

DJ: What does that mean?

SA: Since science has defined its methods as the only way to discover truth, the only acceptable criticisms of science are those conducted within the methodological framework that science has set up for itself. Further, science insists that only those who have been inducted into its community, through means of training and credentials, are qualified to make these criticisms.

But there is something else at stake here. Theirs is a belief in the end of history. It's a version of political economist Francis Fukayama's belief that we've ended history because the world has been unified under the common denominator of capitalism, so-called liberal democracy, the market.

DJ: Obviously there are a lot of problems with Fukayama's boosterism of capitalism, not the least of which is that it doesn't match reality.

SA: Oh, absolutely. His theory makes no sense at all. And the same is true when it is approached scientifically. Some have declared the "end of physics," the title of a recent book by David Lindley; others expand this notion to all of science. The crux of it all is that soon we will understand everything.

DJ: And essentially be as God.

SA: Think about these questions: Does the world change? Is the material world itself moving constantly?

DJ: Absolutely.

SA: If that is true, then we can't ever attain ultimate knowledge. If there exists anything even remotely resembling free-willed actors anywhere in the universe, then there can be no ultimate knowledge of the sort science purports.

Here's the real point. Everybody knows that social and political philosophers generate ideologies. But nobody takes this to be the case for physicists, chemists, or biologists. These people aren't supposed to be dealing in ideology, they're supposed to be dealing with Truth. But they create the myths by which, for better or worse, their work continues. I strongly suspect that there are many of them who, if they didn't believe that they were on the road to Damascus, where they will finally find the Holy Grail of absolute knowledge, would feel they were spinning their wheels. But they want utopia, and the ultimate utopia for science is a unified field theory.

It's all very ideological, but science has a tremendous investment in not being considered ideology. Science actually defines itself as the separation of knowledge from ideology. It's really clever.

The "rigorous" methods of science have become the arbiter of what is real—not speculation, not religious belief, not all the beliefs that existed in the Aristotelian, Ptolomaic, and feudal periods, not direct personal experience. This mythology has seeped into all members of this culture. For example, given a choice between something you experienced and results you are told emerged from a laboratory, which do you believe? Probably the laboratory, because we've been convinced that laboratory experiments show us the world through lenses not "tainted" by emotion, speculation, logic, or ideology.

Scientists won't be able to get away with this forever. It doesn't work, because from the start—while they were developing the scientific method—they already had a priori aims. They had, and continue to have, goals that inform their research. They have subsets of perspectives that include and exclude certain sorts of phenomena.

DJ: I'm getting a little lost.

SA: Let's ground this in biology. We've all heard of the famous monk Gregor Mendel, and we know the Mendel-Morgan hypothesis, which is that the environment exerts almost no long-term influence on human or nonhuman organisms. We know that. I use the word *know*, by the way, ironically. We also know that Jean-Baptiste Lamarck was another nineteenth-century scientist who, even before the founding of modern genetics, repudiated Mendel's underlying premise that organisms respond solely to their inherent genetic makeup. He said that characteristics are not inherited genetically but rather acquired through interactions with one's environment. He believed these characteristics can be passed on to one's progeny. Lamarck's hypothesis was crude, but does that mean Mendel was correct in his notion of genetics?

DJ: Mendel fudged his data, by the way.

SA: Yes, he fudged, and he lied. But that doesn't alter the fact that genetics is now taken as gospel. But what has happened is that as the field of biology, evolutionary biology in particular, has become more sophisticated—due to new theories from people like Luther Burbank; Stephen Jay Gould, whose theory of contingency has challenged the doctrine of adaptation; Francisco Ayala; and Richard Levins—biologists have begun to understand that all organisms exist in context. You cannot understand them out of that context. You cannot take an organism out of its context and have the same organism.

DJ: Of course.

SA: Many biologists are beginning to understand that mutations manifest a relationship with the environment. They're not so much saying this is the case on a one-to-one basis within one generation, but that organisms evolve as adaptations to their environment, and that the environment coadapts to organisms. It's a dialectical or interactive process of mutual determination.

So now there is a big battle going on in biology between the evolutionists and the geneticists, who have radically different theories of organic development. The evolutionists say we have three levels of relationships going on at the same time. One is the relationship an organism has with its own genes, or species have with their genetic pool. The second is the relationship an organism has with its immediate environment. And the third is the relationship an organism has with the whole world. In other words, it's cosmic. This is an ecological perspective, and a brilliant one. Then you have the geneticists, who believe they can put wax moth DNA into cucumbers, or sea cucumber DNA into mice, without larger repercussions. They believe everything is contained in the DNA, that the environment has almost no influence.

Do you want to tell me science isn't ideological, and that scientific research doesn't have a priori aims? I have one word for you: Monsanto. Or make it two words: genetic engineering.

If this fight were going on in the field of physics, by the way, it would never be so openly acknowledged. Biology isn't the emperor of the sciences, like physics. It can afford this sort of battle. But even though it's acceptable to fight this battle in biology, it is still fought very strictly within the confines of the methodology set up by science itself. It's necessarily self-referential.

DJ: No heresy allowed.

SA: Exactly, because from this perspective science is a reflection of the objective world. The propositions of physics, chemistry, biology and so on are by the consensus of the scientific community incontrovertible reflections of reality, or truth.

DJ: I was talking to a scientist friend of mine once about interspecies communication. She was scornful of it. I asked what it would take to convince her, and she said, "If, after you asked it to, the animal did something that was against its nature." Leaving aside the question of what is an animal's nature (determined, of course, by the methodology of science!) I gave her a bunch of examples, both personal and from friends and books. Her face grew more and more set, until at last she said, "There is nothing that you can say that would convince me." That's the power of a dogmatic belief in science.

SA: For some scientists, everything outside the box—defined by the rules of scientific discourse—must be ignored. And I hope you didn't push your friend any further, because sometimes scientists get very agitated when you call them on the game they're playing.

DJ: And the game is?

SA: Religion. Teleology. Control. The desire for prediction, and ultimately the desire to control the natural world, has become the foundation of their methodology of knowing truth.

Think about it. What is a laboratory experiment? At the beginning one must select from the multiplicity of objects and relations that constitute the world a slice to study. To conduct a laboratory experiment the first thing you do is factor out the world. You factor out emotion. You factor out ethics. You factor out nature, if you want to put it that way. You factor out the cosmos. You create a situation of strict abstraction. From that, we think we can extrapolate propositions which correspond to the world and its phenomena. Or rather scientists think that. And these propositions do correspond to the world, so long as we ignore the actual physical world and its context.

DJ: What are the social implications of this?

SA: The point of science—and this may or may not be true of individual scientists—is to make the world subject to human domination. If they can abstract, and then they can predict on the basis of that abstraction, then they can try, at both the human and natural levels, to use that prediction in order to exert control.

Since we already mentioned it, let's use genetic engineering as an example. The ideology underlying its conceptualization is that we cannot and will not depend on nature to yield its own productivity, both in terms of its own development and human need. We're intervening, because the process of maturation has to be faster, the output has to be more plentiful, production has to be cheaper, humans have to be more in control of the process.

DJ: Do you see a difference here between pure and applied science?

SA: First let me say that even within its own framework there is precious little fundamental science going on in America. It's technoscience. For example, elementary particle physicists may or may not need a $3 billion accelerator to continue their research, but Congress turned their proposal down, in part because Congress doesn't think we need any more knowledge of the elementary building blocks of matter. The physics community has been screaming that they can't function without such equipment. What this says to me is that they have tied their science so tightly to technology that it cannot exist without massive influxes of technology and cash.

Because technoscience has gotten so expensive, most scientists can't even get to the point of doing pure research anymore. They're in applied science, or maybe even more likely, product development.

Product development is the key to understanding modern science. Nowadays when scientists apply for funding, whether from corporations or from the National Institutes For Health or the National Science Foundation, they usually have to specify their outcomes in terms of product development. They have to show that their research will lead to a product that's useful to society.

DJ: Unfortunately the same test is not applied to military research, or the whole military-industrial complex would shut down.

SA: True, but the point here is really that a success in any pure or applied science is dependent on the ability to have error, which is not feasible in the realm of product development. Error is the basis of whatever you learn.

DJ: That's as true in life as science.

SA: Yes, but in science, error is regarded as failure. One of the consequences of science increasingly orienting itself to practical outcomes is that at MIT and elsewhere scientists are going straight to the corporations, who let them experiment with this or that problem in molecular biology in exchange for holding the patents of whatever they develop.

DJ: That brings up a more interesting question: what is the relationship between science and capitalism?

SA: Capitalism as we know it couldn't exist without science. And science as we know it has been formed and deformed by capitalism at every step of the way.

The first full-time scientist, by which I mean the first person who was able to make his living with science, was Michael Faraday. He was employed by the Royal Institution in the 1840s to work on electromagnetism. They paid him room and board and a small stipend, and allowed him to entertain people in the upper reaches of society with lectures for which he was paid. One of Faraday's great supporters was Charles Babbage, a very urbane businessman—and the inventor of one of the earliest computers—who was extremely interested in figuring out how science could become fully integrated into industry. Babbage understood that mass production could only become really powerful as a means of making profit and accumulating capital when it became scientifically based. This is far more fundamental than the scientific management movement in which the labor process got chopped up by Taylorism or by Henry Ford using an assembly line. That's part of it. But the use of electricity and machinery changed industry so that instead of drawing a pulley and cutting materials in a factory by hand, you now could install a little electric motor. Chemistry gave industry the Bessemer and the blast furnace.

The upshot of all this is that throughout the nineteenth century science became increasingly vital to capitalism, and then got translated into engineering, which is a practicality-based scientific application. Prior to the 1870s, most engineers were independent contractors, but with the increasing integration of science into industry engineers began to be taken on board as staff. Now engineers are central to most industries; you could almost tell the history of the world since 1850 by the progressive integration of science and engineering into capitalism.

Physics, too, has been crucial to capitalism because of the important advances in communications technologies, many of which were developed not by the government but directly by industry—by the telephone company, for example, or General Electric.

DJ: Where do universities fit into this picture?

SA: That's an interesting question. How did the university get radically transformed from a sleepy trainer for doctors and preachers to its current function as a high-powered scientific-knowledge-based adjunct of capitalism? It was really during the rearmament of 1938, when the United States decided to go to war. That year President Roosevelt appointed Vannevar Bush, a famous scientist, as the first science adviser in the history of the United States. Roosevelt said to him, "Look, we've got to figure out a way to build all these munitions," and Bush did a survey trying to figure out how they were going to do all the research and design for everything from radar to atomic bombs. He decided it would be more efficient and faster to use the preexisting infrastructure of the university system than it would be to build it all from scratch. I just wrote a book on this called *The Knowledge Factory: Dismantling the Corporate University*, and another called *Creating True Higher Learning*.

This transformation of the university system has had immense implications, because it generated an incredibly solid base for the new capitalism: the triumvirate of the university/corporate/government complex. And science is the core of that complex.

The funny part of it all is that none of them look back.

DJ: You wrote something about this that I didn't understand, that "the loss of memory is the transcendental condition for science. A sense of history is inimical to the project of domination because it would generate questions that cannot be answered instrumentally."

SA: Let's discuss this on two levels. First, tell me what it means that you were trained as a physicist. Let me ask you a few questions. What school did you go to?

DJ: The Colorado School of Mines.

SA: Did you ever read Ptolemy?

DJ: Of course not.

SA: You didn't read Aristotle, therefore.

DJ: Correct.

SA: Did you read Galileo Galilee?

DJ: Nope.

SA: Newton?

DJ: Nope.

SA: Anything in the history of science?

DJ: No Descartes, Bacon. Nobody. We didn't read Faraday. We didn't read Einstein. It was purely instrumental.

SA: And if you didn't read about the history of science, you—and I don't mean you personally, but as a cohort, as a generation—never learned that there were fundamental certainties that were completely disrupted. Moreover, you didn't learn that certain things were excluded in the next generation that could have been useful and interesting. That every generation of change excludes and includes—incorporates and marginalizes—certain kinds of knowledges that it doesn't find helpful or useful. You never learned that at one point there were scientific debates, and that the scientific community might or might not have chosen the right side.

DJ: Maybe I've just been dense so far, but I finally get it. If you're going to present your way of knowing as absolute truth, you cannot leave behind evidence of those conflicts. This would explain also why mainstream Christianity always had to mercilessly eradicate all heretical branches, the Albigensians, Anabaptists, and so on.

SA: There's a book called *Leviathan and Air Pump: Hobbes, Boyle and the Experimental Life* about the struggle between Robert Boyle and Thomas Hobbes over what is the nature of scientific knowledge. Hobbes made what would for any red-blooded scientist be an absurd, absolutely bonkers statement: that speculation can be genuine scientific knowledge, that one could draw conclusions about the nature of the universe that were valid through deductive reasoning without the benefit or detriment of observation. Boyle, on the other hand, was a Baconian, who said, "I'm from Missouri; show me. Seeing is believing." And who won out in that battle? Boyle, obviously, who relied on an important article of scientific faith: that reason cannot yield genuine knowledge, that reason is always derivative of observation, and so on.

DJ: But Hobbes's position is absurd, too.

SA: Hold your hesitation for a second. Don't get me wrong. I don't agree with either of these guys. Both sides missed the boat. The same is true for most commentary on their debate. On the one hand we've got Boyle's preference for extremely narrow observations in science, and on the other hand we've got Hobbes's preference for an exclusively intellectual process. The place where Hobbes and Boyle agreed—and I'm not sure either one would have been fully aware of this—was that everything has to be controlled, everything has to be validated through the "mind." The body must be excluded. Ever since the fifteenth and sixteenth centuries we have gone from Cartesianism to Cartesianism.

Let me approach this from another angle. The famous French psychologist and philosopher Maurice Merleau-Ponty said, "The body is a subject." He and philosopher Henri Bergson argued that the body as a feeling subject is a source of knowledge, perhaps the source of knowledge: neither matter nor mind, but energy.

I gain some hope by watching Western medicine's recent discovery of the long Chinese medicinal tradition. Suddenly physicians are acknowledging the effectiveness of acupuncture, and saying, "We don't know why this works." NIH is giving huge grants to try to figure that out. But I'm not sure Western science is up to the task, because acupuncture is based on the notion that the body and the mind are not two separate things, that the brain is not simply a material substance but is something else. It's not ideal and it's not material. And acupuncture is also based on the understanding that feelings—emotions—are real, that the nervous system is connected to our emotions and our health, and that the immune system is linked with our minds and bodies.

Contrast that with our current model, where you go to a finger doctor, a hand doctor, an eye doctor, an ear, nose, and throat doctor. Our bodies have been chopped up like the world is chopped up, and like the assembly line has chopped up our time. Then doctors become specialists in their own particular niches, and the links between nutrition, pollution, how we feel about ourselves—between the totality of our lives and our health—are completely disregarded.

My own doctors over the years have been pretty good people. They do social medicine, they go into the community, they treat the poor. But when I say, "Doc, what do you think about nutrition?" they all say the same thing: "It can't hurt you." "What do you think about vitamins? What do you think about stress?" They shrug. I guess I should be happy that they're open to it at all. But does it have anything to do with their medical practice? Absolutely not.

DJ: Can you tie this back to the question about science requiring no memory?

SA: Science and medicine operate on what I would call an implicit philosophy of the present. That is to say, all that counts is the here and now. Not so much in terms of knowledge, but in terms of politics.

DJ: I'm not sure what you mean by this.

SA: We must be able to continually forget the past and continually reinvent ourselves in order to be able to adapt to the increasingly powerful forces that say that we must subordinate ourselves to the ways of sciences.

The adaptive individual is the one who doesn't have the burden of a past, and who doesn't allow the wider world to impinge upon his or her self-evaluation. Einstein was a person of broad culture. He was tortured by his choices, politicized by them. Many people don't know that Einstein was a communist. And he was. He allowed himself to be aware of history, and he forced himself to deal with the social and moral implications of his scientific—which means political and moral—choices. This led him to an understanding of what he would and would not do.

But science cannot function in the world when it allows itself to fully confront the implications of choices made on a daily basis by scientists. This means that any sort of intensive self-examination simply isn't allowed. If it were allowed the field of science would have to become active. Science as a whole and scientists in particular would have to say, "I refuse to do this. I won't do that. I'm going to become involved not only in the policy of who gets the money, but the policy of what we should be doing."

Self-examination about the horrors created by science in World War II led to a scientists' movement against the bomb. This movement carried through to the 1960s, to the antinuclear movement and the creation of Scientists for Social Responsibility and Engineers for Social Responsibility. But with the exception of climatologists, for example, and a few biologists, particularly conservation biologists, where are the scientists with a conscience now? There are some individuals and organizations in favor of self-examination, but since the Vietnam War the scientific communities of biology, physics, and chemistry have basically surrendered to capital. Their rationalization, that they have to perform services for industry or for the military (which is essentially in service to capitalism) to get any money for research, is absurd.

There are many people who would have been great physicists but who decided in the 1960s that they wouldn't do it. Instead of becoming slaves to capital they became writers, teachers, or professors of humanities. A whole generation said, "We're not going to participate in the war machine, or in the capitalist machine." And they didn't.

DJ: I'm still thinking about this whole question of not having a past, and it occurs to me that if there is no past, there is no accountability.

SA: The question obviously then becomes, are scientists citizens? Or putting it another way, does a citizen have any claims on science? Scientists helped create Three Mile Island. Love Canal. Hanford.

DJ: Global warming.

SA: You can go down the list. Where should we citizens put our words in? How do we hold these scientists accountable for their subordination to capital? Or more specifically, how do we hold them accountable for their subordination to the power of the private corporation?

DJ: What's the answer to that question?

SA: I believe part of the answer is that in a democratic society the citizenry should be broadly educated in science—and I don't mean just the algorithms, the procedures of science alone. I mean the history of science, the politics of science, the culture of science, the ideas of science, and mathematics.

But that is by no means the whole answer. Another part is that we cannot let the scientific community internally police itself any more than we can let General Electric—which is polluting the Albany metropolitan area here in New York—police itself. The Reagan, Bush, and Clinton administrations have pushed this insane policy of having corporations police themselves, and we can all see the disaster that has been for citizens everywhere. We must hold science accountable. We can't depend on politicians.

DJ: I remember a conversation I had with a physicist friend about risk analysis. His stance was that at some point you have to just state that enough mitigation is enough. My response was simple: if scientists state that building a refinery will not cause cancer rates in a community to go up, and then they do, the community should demand a life for a life from the scientists. With their own lives at stake, instead of other peoples' lives, the scientists would not be so cavalier in their service to the corporations. Not surprisingly, my friend was adamantly opposed to that idea.

The stuff we've been talking about is pretty heady; lots of history, lots of philosophy. Why should the person who is honking the horn down on the street right now care about any of this?

SA: The first reason has to do with the person's own life expectancy, and the life expectancies of her or his children. We've got an epidemic of cancer in this country, and it's due to various scientifically-based industries. That epidemic is killing people right now. I would say that's a good enough reason to care.

The second reason is that people increasingly live privatized lives, and that means to a large extent they don't care one way or the other about what we would describe as public affairs. Politics is a very dirty word for many people. But people who understand the meaning of participatory democracy would have to agree that scientific and technological literacy are central to democratic participation in the public life of this society. People have to know enough to be able to intervene at that level. The scientists stand with the government and the corporations, and they are holding the people back. That sounds hortatory, but it's true. The scientific community prevents the American public from intervening in what scientists consider their own private domain. They seem to think we "lay" people are clueless, and we're going to gum up the works. They want us to believe that the triumvirate of government, corporation, and the scientific community will take care of everything and protect us at the same time.

I don't believe them. I don't have that faith in anybody, except people collectively deciding what they want to do within their own lives. And I've got to convince the person who was honking that horn that it's right not to believe them. People should view science with the same skepticism that science holds up as an ideal.

DJ: So you'd like people to understand that the models of science are just that: models. I loved what you wrote about how we should stop using the phrase "laws of nature" and begin using the more accurate phrase "laws of science."

SA: I've gotten all sorts of grief for that statement.

DJ: Why? It cuts to the heart of everything we're talking about.

SA: Let's talk about models. What is a model? A model is an informed ideal type. It is, as Wittgenstein says, a picture of reality in its ideal form. But the problem is that model building is not simply a representation of what we think the world out there looks like. The model becomes increasingly that which we claim is the basis of our prediction and control of the world. Model building has become one of the tools of domination. The best example is the Human Genome Project. They're collecting and classifying many thousands of human genotypes. And they're building models of the human body that are grounded in their classification. To some extent what they have discovered is the result of their model.

DJ: Believing is seeing.

SA: And what are they going to do with this information? Are they going to keep it in the National Archives, like folk music that is collected in the Library of Congress? No. They're going to make it available for people to do genetic engineering, for people who want to "improve the nature of the human species." They're going to use it for the once disgraced pseudoscience of eugenics. They're going to use this to help create the ideal human, with the proper intelligence and the proper looks. And I hate to say this, but you'll be out of luck, Derrick, because you don't have blue eyes.

DJ: My Indian friends hate the Human Genome Product for many reasons, not the least of which is that they believe it will be used to develop diseases that attack specific genome types.

SA: That's the apocalypse.

But we don't even have to look that far away. We can look right outside this window. Right now New York is spraying malathion all over the city.

DJ: I saw a headline today that read, "Let us spray," making the science-religion connection all too clear.

SA: As of the moment we're having this conversation, nine cases of encephalitis, caused by mosquito bites, have been discovered, with fifty more suspected. So how are they dealing with encephalitis, and those mosquitoes? They're spraying everybody with an extremely dangerous chemical. It's going to kill the mosquitoes, but how many kids will it kill over the long run? How many cancer cases will it produce? How many cases of nausea? What will it do to wild bird populations? It's the laboratory model on a huge scale. We will only consider the very specific consequences inside this very little box, and everything else be damned.

It's now coming out that back in the 1950s a doctor did human experiments with what is now called HIV transmitted from chimpanzees. He wanted to conduct his little experiment inside his little theoretical box, and because of that millions of people are dying. And we could say that in some ways his experiment succeeded: he was trying to work on infantile paralysis, and great strides have been made in that area. But at what cost?

DJ: As we talk I keep thinking about the connections between science, capitalism, and Christianity. The central thread that ties them all together is that each one must be the only belief of its type. None of the three will brook any competition.

SA: Monotheism is the scourge of the earth, you know. There can only be one god, one truth, one word, and the word of God is the truth.

DJ: What's so scary about pluralism?

SA: For many people the complexity and confusion of everyday life has to have a resolution in something that they can actually believe in and have faith in. In a way, science is the new faith. It says the buck stops someplace. Like religion, it operates on salvation and redemption. "Better living through chemistry," as Ronald Reagan used to say. Technology will save us from this horrible, insufficient, transient world. And we can redeem ourselves through the technological fix.

DJ: Redeem ourselves from what?

SA: Well, partly from mortality. We can postpone death. We deal with the fear of death through the technological and scientific fix. And we also promise to redeem ourselves from our responsibility to our children and to the future. We tell our children that the future will be taken care of because of the spread of scientific and technological knowledge, and its applications. The horrible irony of this is that in great measure because of science, the world are we leaving for the children is increasingly impoverished and toxic.

DJ: If you could have the readers of this interview take away just one thing from this, what would it be?

SA: That science is simply another form of knowledge. Many scientists consider it absurd that Christian fundamentalists use biblical references to bolster their claim that the Bible is literally true, yet we all let science use the tools of science to settle disputations concerning its own viability. That makes no sense to me.

I need to be clear that I'm not suggesting that science is false.

DJ: I'll do that.

SA: I think science is true. It is a regime of truth for the world in which we live. But it presupposes capitalism. It presupposes the market. It presupposes prediction and control of the world. It presupposes that there be no genuine plurality of ideas about nature. Within that framework it's true, but once you begin to acknowledge that there is more than one way to know the world—and perhaps more importantly, to be in the world—science takes its place among other truths.

JOHN KEEBLE

Interview conducted at
Eastern Washington University,
Spokane, May 26, 2000.

The son of a liberal minister focused on reintegrating urban churches in the 1960s, John Keeble came of age in an environment that was deeply engaged with the civil rights movement. That experience led to a life of investigation into equality, social oppression, class, race, and religion. As he points out, "We live in an entire culture that is racist and afraid, but most of us lie about it." Along with studying hate groups, he has written extensively on the oil industry. To Keeble, the connections are obvious; both entities exploit and oppress communities, seeking, as Keeble puts it, "the intrusion of exploitative and oppressive institutions onto landscapes and communities." Hate groups and corporations have the same objective, namely, "to turn everyone and everything into objects."

Keeble is the author of four novels, including *Yellowfish* and *Broken Ground*, and a work of nonfiction, *Out of the Channel: The Exxon Valdez Oil Spill in Prince William Sound*. His collection of stories, *Nocturnal America*, the winner of the Prairie Schooner Book Prize in Fiction, was released by the University of Nebraska Press in 2006. His fiction and nonfiction have appeared in periodicals and anthologies, including *Outside*, the *Village Voice*, *American Short Fiction*, *Prairie Schooner*, *Northwest Review*, *Zyzzyva*, *Idaho Review*, and *Best American Short Stories*. He has received a Guggenheim Fellowship, a Pulitzer nomination for his *Village Voice* piece "Black Spring in Valdez," and an Emmy nomination for *To Write and Keep Kind*, a documentary film on the life of Raymond Carver.

He is a longstanding member of the MFA faculty at Eastern Washington University. He has also served as the Visiting Chair in Creative Writing at the University of Alabama on three separate occasions, Visiting Professor of Creative Writing for one additional year at Alabama, and as Distinguished Visiting Writer at Boise State University. He and his family live in Eastern Washington, where they operate a farm.

Derrick Jensen: Why have you spent so many years studying white supremacist groups?

John Keeble: My interest in supremacist groups goes back to my adolescence in the 1960s and has all along been both personal and ideological, or civic. It's personal in the sense that I'm the son of a minister who was left of center and who spent a fair amount of his professional life involved with churches in urban centers that had gone through a period of decay. His job was to "reintegrate" the churches, to inhabit them with people who lived in the neighborhood, as opposed to having the churches run by people who had fled to the suburbs. When I was in junior high and high school my father was involved in a major battle with a right-wing group, the John Birchers, who controlled the church from a distance. I remember my mother receiving graphic death threats over this, and I remember her attempting suicide. My father's efforts ultimately failed, as the John Birchers maintained control of the church. There was a takeover of the region's churches in general by the far right. These far-right groups appealed to members of the lower-middle and upper-lower classes.

In the late 1980s I began to notice the Aryan Nations, a white supremacist group with its headquarters just across the border in Hayden Lake, Idaho, receiving some local press. I was disturbed by the left-wing response to the Aryan Nations; it seemed that the left-wingers were attempting to silence them. I've always believed that the First Amendment is our most important, and if we begin to limit what people can speak or think, everything good about our culture will be lost. As a citizen I consider it part of my job to defend the right of anyone to speak, no matter how painful that may be. So, paradoxically, I became very interested in defending the free speech rights of Aryan Nations members. This was true not only as a matter of principle, but also as a matter of practicality, because every time they speak, we all benefit.

DJ: How?

JK: Two ways. The first is that the Aryan Nations and other white supremacist groups articulate racist and deranged right-wing religious values as well as anyone does, and understanding their perspective is critical to resisting them. But there's another, much deeper, point to be made here, which is that they admit that they're racist and afraid. We live in an entire culture that is racist and afraid, but most of us lie about it. So the obvious racism and fear that characterizes these groups gives us a sort of fingerhold by which we can pry our way into understanding the racism that forms the soft white underbelly of our culture. I don't think we can understand our own racism unless it is brought into the light.

Have you heard about the Aryan Nations parades in Coeur d'Alene, Idaho? Each year there are tremendous controversies over whether the parades should be granted permits. It probably won't surprise you, but I think the Aryan Nations should be allowed to march. This is not only because of what I mentioned before, but also because Coeur d'Alene is attempting to turn itself into an upper-middle-class resort, with enormous amounts of money being poured into wastage of various types—for example, an opulent hotel and a golf course with a floating tee in the middle of a lake. In many ways that makes Coeur d'Alene the best place in the world for the Aryan Nations to march on the Fourth of July. The Coeur d'Alene basin has been laid to waste ever since the Europeans arrived, first by mining companies, then lumber companies. Now, having exhausted those possibilities, entrepreneurs want to turn the region into a "destination resort." There are many reasons for this, primary among them that Coeur d'Alene remains, so long as you don't venture too far from the main highways and into the clearcuts, an absolutely beautiful place. But to the degree that these entrepreneurs succeed, all of the North Idaho Panhandle will be taken over by the rich. It is already a place for white people to go; the three counties of the Idaho Panhandle have less than 3 percent nonwhite populations. I think this whiteness is one of the attractions for a lot of the middle and upper-middle class and very rich people moving into the area. Of course most of them wouldn't admit it. But because of this unacknowledged attraction, the Aryan Nations and the groups like them are precisely the kind of publicity that the region's entrepreneurs do not want.

DJ: How does this relate to big oil, the other subject you've studied throughout your career?

JK: In 1987 I published a novel called *Broken Ground* which had as its subject the construction of a prison for profit. One of the things I attempted to deal with in that novel was the relationship between a place and the residents of that place on one hand, and on the other the superimposition of a big construction project that was oppressive and opportunistic on several different levels at once. I had these issues in mind while I worked on the Aryan Nations project.

In 1989, the Exxon Valdez oil spill occurred in Prince William Sound. I went to the site, and I knew the moment I stepped off the plane that I was involved in oil for the long haul. It was immediately apparent that all of the things that already preoccupied me were in play: capitalist opportunism, racism (manifested here in the form of the relations between whites and indigenous people), and damage to the environment. These were all unfolding before me in the form of a story.

In a very brief time span the oil spill recapitulated the history of serious pollution in the West. The Love Canal toxic waste controversy took years to unfold, the Hanford Nuclear Reservation's impact will take centuries, and the decimation of the continent's forests has been proceeding apace for several hundred years now. But the Exxon Valdez spill made its kill in two weeks. For me it became a parable in which the nation's history of environmental destruction was condensed, its components made clear: the cause, the initial devastation, the continuing effects, the institutionalization of remedies, the denial, the propaganda, and ultimately, the forgetfulness.

Now at last we get to the murky and necessarily unacknowledged relationship between transnational corporations and hate groups. They are branches from the same tree, different forms of the same cultural imperative.

DJ: Which is?

JK: To rob the world of its subjectivity. To turn everyone and everything into objects.

The methodology used by each is different. Corporations are carriers of ruin, turning everything they touch to money. They are culturally sanctified, supported, and protected in their role of turning the living—forests, oceans, mountains, rivers, human lives—into the dead: money. And because they are culturally sanctified they get to act above ground.

DJ: And hate groups?

JK: Beneath, hidden, hated. But they serve that same function of objectifying. Their entire self-definition is based on this objectification.

I can hate another person because of who he is without denying his individuality. In fact, it's possible to hate him because of who he is. But if I hate a person because she's black, or an Indian, or a Jew, or a woman, or a homosexual, I'm not even giving her the honor of hating her in particular. I'm hating a stereotype that I'm projecting onto her.

DJ: That movement toward depriving others of their subjectivity is the central movement of our culture. Indian after Indian has told me that the most basic difference between Western and Indigenous ways of being is that Westerners view the world as dead, not filled with speaking, thinking, feeling, subjects as worthy and valuable as themselves.

JK: Corporations and hate groups have something else in common: they both operate under extraordinary illusion. For example, individual members of an oil company don't connect their work to environmental ruin. They're merely attempting to maximize profits, and in so doing they talk themselves into committing the most horrible of atrocities. It is difficult to think our way through something we're inside of. That's where hate groups come in. They are the hidden underside of the same motivations, living, breathing shadows of European history on this continent. Because they admit their hatred more or less openly, we get to hate them—hate these hate groups—for their heavy handed, comic-book propaganda, and especially for the hatred that is there in the culture, but which we cannot acknowledge. And that's too bad, because a threat unacknowledged is ultimately—on a bone level—far more disturbing than an acknowledged and understood threat. Of course it's also more dangerous. This is true whether we're talking about something as simple and as easy to fix as a broken stair step, or something as convoluted and confusing as an abusive family, or an abusive culture.

This all takes us firmly into the world of illusion. In the case of a white supremacist, the role of illusion is fairly clear. The religious ideology of white supremacist hate groups is based on the notion that all Aryans, so-called, are descended from Abel, and all people of color are descended from Cain. From there it spreads out in an extremely elaborate and exotic fashion to include such details as the idea that Queen Elizabeth is the direct descendant of Adam and presently occupies the throne of Israel. There is an ideological and belief-based complex of illusions that provides them with the ground upon which they can act.

DJ: Before you began writing about hate groups, you were interested in prisons. It seems clear that if you go just by the numbers, the largest, most effective racist group in the country is the American judicial/penal system, because it has achieved segregation on a scale the KKK could only dream of.

JK: They make the KKK and the Aryan Nations seem like child's play.

DJ: The journalist Christian Parenti said American prisons operate on a model that emerged from the Southern slave camps.

JK: It's not surprising that hate groups emerged from the same area. After the Civil War, the KKK enjoyed immense popular support, springing up almost overnight into a huge grassroots organization. I believe that happened in part because the Southerners were a defeated people. So they created what Foucault would call spectacles of terror against what they perceived as an enemy who was both potent and impotent. Potent as a possibility, and functionally relatively impotent. So it's kind of obvious how that would happen.

That process of enslavement of nonwhites continued in the west, with penal colonies where native people were set to work on agriculture. Private prisons were common in the late 1800s and early 1900s, rationalized by the same argument used to rationalize private prisons today, which is that if something is produced, prisons will pay for themselves.

DJ: That sounds like slavery all over.

JK: It is slavery. That was the argument of *Broken Ground*, insofar as the novel had an argument. When people who transgress are simply passed over to an institution that doesn't have any significant moral or community obligations, and is simply going to use the bodies it cages as a means of making money, it creates in the public a kind of disengagement, an open invitation for institutionalized denial. The public is absolved from the pain of either caring for or rehabilitating those members of its own body who have in some way transgressed.

DJ: You said, "Insofar as the novel has an argument." That makes me wonder, what's the relationship between a writer and justice?

JK: Years ago I heard the poet Ed Dorn give a long riff on how the role of a writer is to be a record keeper. That impressed and liberated me. It opened me up, and I could see a way of thinking about writing that doesn't eliminate but certainly limits the role of personal ego. So often young writers are wrapped up in whatever successes they may or may not have, but if you're a record keeper, those concerns begin to vanish. You are faced with attempting to record the complexity of a world that is far more complex than you think. Writing is a way of creating a kind of invitation for readers to engage in that complexity.

DJ: Milan Kundera wrote that the struggle against power is the struggle of memory against forgetting.

JK: That's absolutely true. The record must be kept; oppression, and the alienating effect of oppression, causes forgetfulness. When you are alienated from the world, you become alienated from yourself, and you forget things that are critical to your being.

Say I hit you and take your cash every day at ten o'clock. If I can get you to forget, you'll keep carrying cash and keep walking up to me. But if you remember, you're going to walk down a different street, or maybe you'll carry a gun and shoot me. So on a real basic level, it's in the interests of those in power . . .

DJ: To get us to forget . . .

JK: That they're robbing us time and again.

So you keep the record to remember what injustice was done, or what justice was done, so you can see what happened, and so you can learn.

It is important to remain aware that we're in the practice of keeping records while we're doing it, and to make our records accurate, fair, and complete. I studied Father Serra in junior high and high school in Southern California. He was a heroic figure, my class learned, who founded the California mission system. But we were never taught that he regularly beat his Indian prisoners, nor that the mission system was part and parcel of a genocidal project. Why did we not learn that, and what does our ignorance cost us? If we get into the habit of either ignoring or destroying records of the past, then it's logical to begin to assume that records of the present aren't important. It's bad enough to go back to a text and discover that Father Serra was an asshole. It's much worse to be the person writing such a text now.

DJ: It seems to me that my job as a writer is to articulate that which I know in my heart to be true, and in so doing help others to articulate their own truths.

JK: That's good. The challenge is to form how you feel, how you're responding to things as an animal, as an organism, into something that is coherent and moral.

DJ: Some writers are very adamant that writers not be activists.

JK: I disagree with that position completely, because I think writers are always advocates. Simply by choosing one detail over another you are advocating. I think it's a mistake not to be conscious that you are doing this as you are writing. The challenge is to prevent ourselves from being lazy when we're making a story, and using whatever comes easy to us, or whatever has been handed to us by our culture, without considering what it means. That's what's difficult.

DJ: That brings us back to the question of taking in lies. What does it mean when we take for granted that politicians and corporations lie to us?

JK: Many would say that the lies are necessary, that they have no significant ill effects on the landscapes of our hearts or the wild. When the truth leaks in, we're faced with our own mortality, which most people in this society go to great lengths to avoid. I use cataclysms a lot in my writing to explore what happens when we can't avoid reality. Natural disasters cut through the lies and put people in touch with their nature in ways that everyday life in this culture doesn't.

Experiencing danger and ugliness without the false security our illusions provide can be terrifying, yes. But only when we find the courage to live in truth can we begin to clear the path to environmental and social justice.

LUIS RODRIGUEZ

Interview conducted
in Chicago, May 1, 1999.

In his autobiographical book *Always Running: La Vida Loca, Gang Days in L.A.*, Luis Rodriguez describes an incident that makes clear the violent reality of his childhood in the barrios of Los Angeles. When Rodriguez was ten, he and his friend Tino went to play basketball outside a local school one evening. A police car pulled up, and the officers yelled for them to come over to the car. When the boys refused, the police chased them. Trying to get away, Tino climbed atop the school, fell through a skylight, and died.

Tino was not the only person Rodriguez saw die. By the time he turned eighteen, twenty-five of his friends had been killed by rival gangs, police, drugs, car crashes, and suicides. Rodriguez's experience isn't unique. From 1990 to 1998, for example, more than six thousand Los Angeles youths were killed in gang-related incidents.

Rodriguez believes that addressing this problem by criminalizing those society cannot accommodate, outlawing their actions, and declaring them the enemy is exacerbating the problem. "These people against whom we are waging war," he writes, "are children who ultimately want what any child wants: respect, protection, and belonging. Children who join gangs want the same things as children who join the YMCA, Little League, or the Boy Scouts. What does society provide them with instead? Within a three-mile radius of South Central Los Angeles, there are 640 liquor stores, but not one movie theater or community center." As Rodriguez points out, "gangs flourish when there's a lack of social recreation, decent education, or employment. Today, many young people will never know what it is to work. They can satisfy their needs only through collective strength—against the police, who hold the power of life and death; against poverty; against idleness; against their impotence in society."

Born in the United States of Mexican parents, Rodriguez spent his early childhood in Mexico. Later, when his family immigrated to the U.S., he joined a gang. He and his fellow gang members saw no future outside their community. "We were kind of confined to a world," he says. "The sense was you couldn't get out of this world. You were supposed to conform to the poverty, to the factories, to whatever people said—this was our lot."

Rodriguez left the gang life behind in large part because, as he writes, "poetry allowed me to see beyond that." He attended high school close to where his father worked, and after school he would wait at a nearby college library for his father to get off so they could go home together. To kill time, Rodriguez browsed the stacks, and that's where he discovered the literature of revolution: Claude Brown's *Manchild in the Promised Land*, the works of Haki Madhubuti and Amiri Baraka, and, most important to him, Piri Thomas's *Down These Mean Streets*. He eventually dropped out of school and ended up back on the streets, but, he writes, "it wasn't the same as before. A power pulsed in those books I learned to savor, in the magical hours I spent in the library—and it called me back to them."

In part because of the violence Rodriguez committed in his youth, he has "sentenced" himself, as he puts it, to a lifetime of community service. He serves through his art, giving readings and workshops at prisons and elsewhere, and through the organization Youth Struggling for Survival, which he founded in order to help young people leave behind violence and find meaning. He is the author of three books of poetry—*Poems across the Pavement, The Concrete River*, and *Trochemoche*, and the children's books *It Doesn't Have to Be This Way* and *America Is Her Name*. He also runs Tia Chucha Press, which is dedicated to publishing socially conscious poets.

I interviewed Rodriguez on Labor Day in Chicago, not too far from Haymarket Square, where a tiny marker commemorates the labor activists whose executions in 1886 led to the creation of the original labor holiday. We sat in Rodriguez's small but comfortable living room and talked of what it would mean to stop thinking of gang members as criminals and start seeing them as children and young men and women, the future of our communities. As we spoke, his five-year-old son sat on the couch behind him, occasionally peeking around at me.

Derrick Jensen: In your book *Always Running: La Vida Loca, Gang Days in L.A.*, you wrote that gang violence in the 1960s was only the beginning of "a consistent and growing genocidal level of destruction predicated on the premise that marginalized youth with no jobs or future are therefore expendable."

Luis Rodriguez: When I was growing up in the 1960s, only a few people were dedicated to living "the crazy life." It wasn't for everybody. For the most part, those who lived it were troubled kids who looked at the dark side of life and were willing to do things most people probably wouldn't—to break boundaries and become outlaws. We didn't want everybody in the gang; we wanted only the ones who'd manifest a kind of craziness, who'd be loco, who were what they now call *caga palos*: really hard.

But in the last thirty years, many more people have become economically marginalized. And once you're economically marginalized, you're marginalized in every other way, too. L.A. provides a good example of this. Many Mexicans moved there to work in the factories and sweatshops, but in the 1970s and 1980s, all the big shops, steel mills, auto plants, and meatpacking plants began shutting down. Whole communities built on these industries suffered, and the kids in these communities grew up not only unable to go to college, but unable even to get a job. They started feeling expendable. And when you see yourself as expendable—when you've been told often enough that you are expendable—it's very easy to "go crazy."

It's the same here in Chicago, which used to be a big industrial city. The industry has fled, and the kids—whether African-American, Puerto Rican, Mexican, or poor white—are all going crazy. They even acknowledge this in the names of their gangs: the Insane Nations, the Maniacs. And it's not happening just in big cities, but in the cornfields of Nebraska and in small towns in Wisconsin.

DJ: What's the connection between economic marginalization and marginalization in other areas?

LR: Our culture's value system is built around being "productive," which is defined as having a job. Even if you're poor, when you're employed you have a sense of being valuable in society. When your job disappears because of new technology or moving factories to Central America, it's easy to internalize that feeling of worthlessness, instead of connecting your personal experience to larger economic and social issues.

I contend that "productivity" is the right way for society to measure a person's value, but that doesn't alter the fact that if you've got 70 percent unemployment on the west side of Chicago, that's a large group of people who have "no value" to society. And if you have no value to society, everything else follows right behind: schools don't bother to educate you. Cops beat you up. Eventually, society puts you in prison to get you out of the way.

Young people, whether or not they're working, have to be given a sense of who they are and be presented with the opportunity to do something with themselves. So often, when these kids turn violent, we see it as a behavior issue, and the kids themselves often feel they're going crazy, that there's something wrong with them. But there are plenty of larger problems that these kids are merely expressing.

DJ: Reading your book, I was struck by how incomprehensibly different our childhoods were.

LR: My family moved from Mexico to a very poor, predominantly black and Mexican neighborhood in South Central L.A., and the first time my siblings and I walked up the street, we got beaten up. Then there were railroad tracks we had to be sure not to cross, because whites lived on the other side, and if we crossed the tracks, they would beat us up. No matter where we went, someone was waiting to hurt us, to make sure we understood our place and how the world worked. In such an environment, we learned quickly that the world was full of limitations. We didn't cross the tracks. We didn't cross certain streets. We didn't take certain classes. Teachers constantly told us to shut up, told us we'd never amount to anything. They told us not to speak Spanish. If we did, they'd hit us.

I grew up going to church, and my mother and father were fairly good parents, so it was hard for me to believe the world could be as violent as it seemed. Even by the time I was ten, when I had already seen so much violence, I didn't quite believe it was real until the evening my friend Tino and I went to play basketball, some cops chased us, and Tino fell through a skylight and died.

I ran from the cops that evening not so much because I was afraid, but because Tino said they would beat us up, and because he ran. I couldn't quite make the connection between playing basketball and getting beaten up. But there the cops were, chasing a couple of kids whose only crimes were shooting baskets and being poor and Mexican.

My family was always dislocated. We never fit in. No matter how many barriers we crossed, there were always more in front of us. Even when we later moved to the San Gabriel Valley, the schools there had a tracking system. (It's illegal, but it still exists.) If you were Mexican and from my barrio, the Lomas, you were put in what they called the "stupid classes." If you tried to break out of that track, they found ways to keep you in your place. I tried to take classes in art, photography, and literature, but the counselor told me those classes were all full. It was always the same: "I think you'll find our industrial arts classes more suited to your needs." We were to work with our hands. They were preparing us to be factory workers.

Growing up in these circumstances, it was easy to become violent and rageful. I don't think that's an unreasonable—or unexpected—response. If you're treated like an outlaw, why not be one, even be proud of it? So by the time you're, say, eleven, you're starting your own gang. It was a way for us to belong to something, to embrace ourselves when others beat us.

You might ask where our families were during all this. Our parents were working hard just to stay alive and were unable to see what was happening. My mom and dad were good people, but they couldn't handle the difficult questions we brought them. When we told them the cops were beating us up, they couldn't believe it. "What are you talking about?" they said. In Mexico, maybe, but not in the U.S. Not here.

So where could we go? All the adults denied what we were experiencing every day. So we had to create our own little world where only we could speak the language, and where we could define our own values, define ourselves. Then we could say, "We don't care about your values," and scare those who were prejudiced against us. That's a big reason we tattooed ourselves and walked a certain walk and wore certain kinds of clothing. We wanted people to know we were coming, and we wanted to say to them, "You may not respect us, but you're going to fear us."

DJ: Years ago, I asked Ward Churchill why oppressed groups so often turn to violence, and he said, "If you tell people they're insignificant long enough, they may one day prove their significance by blowing your brains out."

LR: I think that's hard for people to accept, because not everyone has felt the kind of deep meaninglessness that can bring you to that level. But it does happen.

DJ: So how do these gangs end up shooting mostly at each other?

LR: I think it starts with self-hate. When you're given so little esteem by society at large, your social club becomes your only source of real pride: these are my "homies," and we've got our jackets, and we've got our name—the Gents, Kings, Superiors, Regents, Chancellors. We gave ourselves those grand names because we wanted to lift ourselves up. But all the time, self-hatred was festering underneath, because no matter how much pride we tried to build up, there was still that nagging voice saying, You ain't no good, you ain't no good. And so, eventually, we turned on each other. Our biggest enemy became not the police, the teachers, or the white guys, but each other.

DJ: But why?

LR: Let's say you've got your social club, and you're really proud of it. Now you and your homies go to a party wearing your jackets, and you look across the room, and you see another group of guys wearing their jackets. You're mirror images of each other. They look like you, and you look like them. They act like you, and you act like them. You hate yourself, and you hate them. You feel as if they're moving in on your party. So you challenge them, or they challenge you. It escalates. You fight them, and if one of them beats you up, you get five other guys to beat him up. All anyone has to do is throw a gun into the mix, and pretty soon somebody will use it. And once one side uses a gun, the other has to use a gun to pay them back. So it doesn't take long for kids who are suicidal, self-hating, and on the edge of madness to start killing each other.

DJ: You've written that "there is an aspect of suicide in young people whose options have been cut off. They stand on street corners, flashing hand signs, inviting the bullets."

LR: Before we explore this further, I want to say that not every kid in a gang is violent. Most join just because it's their neighborhood gang, their friends are in it, and they want protection. Ninety percent of what gangs do is hang out. What we've been told about these kids being "super-predators" is a myth. Most of what they do is boring, boring, boring.

But within each gang, there will often be a hardcore group of people who are violent. Maybe they've been beaten up by their dads, or by cops, or they've seen too much violence in the street. Whatever the reason, they're in a gang and they've got all this hatred, so eventually the gang becomes the place where they can lash out at the world for everything it has done to them.

What they're doing, though, is not just homicidal but suicidal. They're killing people just like themselves, and they're setting themselves up to be killed the same way. They hope to die in a blaze of glory. All other value has been taken away from them, but at least they can die for their barrio. It's a very heroic stance. I know because I used to take it. I would shoot at members of other gangs, but I would also challenge them: "Come and shoot me." It's all connected. You want to kill them, but you also want them to kill you.

DJ: Is this reasoning conscious?

LR: Very rarely. I try to explain it to the gang members I work with, and sometimes they agree. "I never thought of it that way," they say.

These suicidal impulses don't emerge on their own. Society encourages these kids to turn their hatred inward because otherwise there's a strong possibility they would turn their rage against the system. This is where the police often come in. Sometimes their methods are as obvious as taking members of one gang over to another gang's territory and forcing them to paint over that gang's graffiti. But often it's subtler than that. All you need to do is facilitate the flow of weapons and drugs into the community.

Now, people may find this hard to believe.

DJ: "Not in the U.S.," as your parents would have said.

LR: Exactly. But it's been proven that this happens. Usually you can't pinpoint it, because the cops are smart enough to use indirect means. But they allow certain things to happen that will turn kids against each other.

DJ: A couple of years ago, I read an article in which the lead singer of the rock group Rage against the Machine called the police "the biggest and most violent gang in the country."

LR: That's the way we saw it, and that conclusion is easy to come to: They've got the guns. They've got the uniforms. They've got the talk. Often they even have gang names.

The interesting thing is that the gangs and the cops need each other. The gang member and the cop are practically created from the same cloth. Cops are marginalized in our society, in that they're assigned to deal with the people nobody else wants to deal with. Nobody wants to give these kids jobs, psychological counseling, a proper education, spiritual engagement—anything they really need. So society says to the cops, "You take care of them." And the cops believe they really are the "thin blue line" that separates this "garbage" from the rest of society.

Cops go crazy, too. I'm sure you've heard about the high rates of abuse, alcoholism, and suicide among police. Why does that happen? Because despite all the cop shows and movies idealizing the police, they are in no way capable of handling the problems society has abdicated to them.

The gang kids end up paying the highest price. Society says they're the enemy, so the police beat them up and harass them and even kill them, or put them in prison for almost nothing. All because society doesn't want to deal with their problems.

Once I was at a retreat, and a gang member got up and said to one of the white guys there, "My friend was killed by the cops, and I hate white people." The white guy responded, "I had nothing to do with it."

I think they were both missing the point. The kid wasn't focusing on the real economic and social issues, and the white guy was forgetting that there are many people living in the suburbs, and especially in gated communities, who have removed themselves from the larger community, and who demand that cops "take care of" inner-city kids. Clearly, when a kid gets killed by a cop, the resident of the gated community is not pulling the trigger, but he or she has helped make that kid's death possible—and in some ways inevitable. The police are killing inner-city kids in the name of protecting that gated community.

Now, I don't hate cops. In fact, I feel bad for them the same way I feel bad for these kids. We're setting both groups up. They're all caught in the same web.

DJ: What is that web?

LR: It starts with social pathologies. The pathologies may be violence at home, violence in the community, or whatever. But society is not entirely to blame. Much of the responsibility lies with the person who is caught in the web.

If you go into a prison, you'll see that many gang members, especially the Mexicans, have spiderweb tattoos. If you ask them why, they'll say, "Society is coming at me, and I'm caught in the middle." What I say to them is "You, too, are creating the web. No matter what society has done, no matter how marginalized you are—economically, socially, psychologically—you've got to identify with that role in order for the trap to work. La vida loca is a web that you've spun yourself. You've created your own prison. Yes, what happened to you was awful, inexcusable, but that pathology stays with you only if you socialize yourself around it. It's up to you to stop identifying with these roles that society has thrust upon you."

Of course, the answer is not to pretend the pathology doesn't exist, that you're not actually caught in any web, that you don't or shouldn't feel anger. If something happened in your life or in your family that really hurt you, that caught you in its pathology, then you have to go through those wounds to be renewed, to be reborn out of it. There's a saying, "The wound is the womb." We all have to be reborn. And that's true not just of troubled young people, but of everyone, at every stage of life.

Native cultures are rich with initiations and rites of passage. A big reason kids get into gangs is because our society doesn't provide them with initiation rituals that are meaningful to them, that validate who they are and what they feel. So they create their own rites of passage, but their rites are not complete because they don't come from a larger communal tradition, and they aren't validated by society. In fact, they're explicitly invalidated: "How could you possibly join a gang?"

People generally don't see the initiation role of these gangs. Or of prison. Prison is a profound initiation, an experience intense enough to get anyone to renew themselves. But again, it's completely invalidated. The community condemns the offender, the jury convicts him, the judge sentences him, and the cops are there throughout the process. But after the kid has done his time—when he returns to the community—nobody is there for him. All those people who were so adamant about putting him away have moved on. There's no follow-up. So the potential rite of passage is invalidated by society, and most kids end up going back to prison, where their experience is valid. It's the same with the gangs: if the larger community doesn't validate and recognize what these young people are trying to do, they'll keep going back until they're either in prison, dead, or addicted to drugs.

DJ: I wonder if part of these kids' suicidal impulse comes from confusing actual physical death with the need to end one way of life so that another can be born.

LR: What has to die if you're going to be reborn is your infantile ego. Its death is necessary and natural. But you're right, kids don't understand that. They believe you really have to die. These kids need to die symbolically, but they're doing it for real because nobody's explained to them what they're going through.

Another reason these kids are so violent is that they pick up and distort certain values of mainstream society: "Survival of the fittest." "Kill or be killed." Gang members always say these things. Expressions like these are capitalism in a nutshell, the whole social order. You go to the stock market floor or the boardroom, and you'll see "kill or be killed" in action.

If you think about it, many of these gangs are creating little capitalist systems in their own marginalized, impoverished ways. Drugs becomes their industry, and they literally "kill or be killed" to make the sales. They become very adept capitalists, but, just as with their initiation rituals, their business ventures aren't legitimized by society as a whole, so they aren't able to invest or hold on to the money, which means they won't have much to show for all their years in business. They've bought into the whole system, yet they're deprived of what they need most, which is social recognition. So they stay in their own destructive business and often end up in prison. Prison is full of entrepreneurs who, in another environment, would have been thriving capitalists. They're the first ones to tell you, "I was just trying to make money."

I remember one time I went to a juvenile hall and read some poetry. Afterward, one guy got up and asked, "Is there money in poetry?"

"Actually, there is," I said, "but that's not why I do it. I do it because I have the love and the calling."

He said, "Forget that stuff. If it don't make dollars, it don't make sense."

I thought, "Who taught him that?" The truth is that we all taught him that. Every commercial and program on TV, every message our society sends pushes him in that direction. He's just trying to be a part of society. The problem is that he'll never be a part of it. Instead of being a pillar of the community, he's in prison.

DJ: Given this society's value structure and the reality of 30–70 percent unemployment in some communities, what can we do to keep fifteen-year-old kids from killing each other?

LR: It's hard. When I was growing up, I would have shot anybody I thought was in my way. But I matured. That's another thing most people don't realize about gang members: most of them don't get killed; they just mature. They start a family or start working, and they begin to think, "Well, this ain't the way to go. I'm tired of shooting people and seeing my friends get shot."

But how do we save the kids? We change society. And that's where it gets hard. As long as we have an industrial economy, we aren't going to get far. It's industry that created gangs, because industry invented unemployment. The first street gangs we know of came into being in England during the Industrial Revolution. Soon after that, they appeared in the industrialized parts of the U.S., like New York City, for example, where immigrants came to work in the sweatshops. The first U.S. gangs were composed mainly of Irish immigrant kids. Later gangs were made up of Eastern European immigrants, then Jewish immigrants, then Italian immigrants. Like the gangs of today, these gangs had colors and names, and there were gang wars and rumbles. In fact, the most devastating gang rumble ever recorded wasn't between the Bloods and the Crips but between the Dead Rabbits and the Bowery Boys—two Irish immigrant gangs in Hell's Kitchen. The fighting lasted several days and left a hundred casualties, including at least a dozen dead and several cops shot.

So gangs are products of the industrial age, which is largely over. Unfortunately, the end of the industrial age doesn't mean the end of gangs. The last time we had a shift of this magnitude was more than a hundred years ago, when the U.S. transformed from a plantation-agricultural society into an industrial society. That transition unleashed all sorts of chaos, and we're going through the same thing now with the switch to a technological, information-based economy. This new economy is unable to integrate everybody, so we're seeing a whole layer of society that doesn't quite fit into the capitalist system anymore. Now we've got to figure out what to do with these people.

Gangs have exploded all over the country. And it's not just black and brown kids anymore. The fastest rise in gang membership is among whites. I did a reading in a coal-mining town in eastern Ohio. The mines and mills there had all shut down, and the families whose grandfathers and great-grandfathers and great-great-grandfathers had worked in those mines and mills now had nothing. Two hundred kids showed up at my reading, all white. And they were really into what I was saying. If I'd closed my eyes, it could have been South Central Los Angeles or the west side of Chicago. They listened to heavy metal instead of rap, but they were all out for revolution, just like kids in Los Angeles. They had nothing to believe in and nowhere to go. Unfortunately, many of them were messed up on drugs—methamphetamines. That's when I began to see that the problems don't break down along racial lines, but have to do with fundamental economic changes.

In order to turn this period of change into something positive, we've got to undermine the logic of capitalism and reclaim whatever remnants of community we still have. Community has never been what capitalism says it is: a conglomeration of discrete individuals all pulling in their own selfish directions. Real community has always been made up of families, or just people, coming together for the benefit of everyone. It's based on the premise that the survival of the community depends on the flowering of all of its members. In order for capitalism really to take hold as it has, that kind of community had to be discarded, discredited, and forgotten for many generations and replaced with dog-eat-dog nonsense. So now we have to revive the old ways again.

Gang members are striving for some kind of genuine community, one that will care for them, that won't just let them slide or punish them. They want a community that addresses their souls, that gives their lives meaning. Every community that seeks to reestablish itself needs to start asking how it can bring purpose and meaning back into the lives of its children.

DJ: So how do we do that?

LR: First, by recognizing that these kids are assets to the community. They're not empty vessels that we have to pour resources into. They're born with gifts, and all they need is enough nurturing and support to make it through the early stages of life and become competent and confident human beings. That is what creates community. You're not going to create community out of a bunch of disconnected, wounded, maimed, hurting people, which is what we already have.

Every stage of a person's life brings different developmental needs, and a real community intervenes appropriately at every stage. But that's not happening in our society. For example, when you're twenty years old, you're approaching a major crossroads in your life, but by that age, most of these gang members are put away in prison and forgotten. Never mind putting kids in adult prisons; I don't think twenty-year-olds should be put away at all, because there's still time to change their lives. Huge changes take place in the early twenties.

It may be a cliché, but kids really are our future. We've lost that basic human understanding, but we can learn it again. It comes back if we just let it. It's what my friend the mythologist Michael Meade calls "bone memory."

I do poetry workshops with kids in prison. Many of them say, "I don't want to write a poem." I tell them just to write randomly, and I give them suggestions to help push them. When they write, all the memories start coming back. They're astounded. They didn't know they had it in them.

We try to teach these kids that their creativity is inexhaustible. It's a lesson that can save their lives. They want to die because they're in a box and don't know how to get out of it. In prison, they're condemned to being useless, and they need to know that they're still useful in the world, that they can still have some impact through their creativity. They need to learn that, no matter how constricted their external circumstances may become, their creativity is boundless.

I'm no expert on Carl Jung, but I like his idea of the collective unconscious: that we all have an ancestral pool of knowledge and experience that we've somehow forgotten about. We tend to think everything is unique to us, and some of it is, but a lot of it is common to the human experience. And we can tap into that shared source.

We often do sweat lodge ceremonies with gang members, especially Mexicans, because in their bones these kids are indigenous people. Part of why they are so wounded and violent is that they've been de-Indianized. So we work with indigenous elders to try to burn away five hundred years of colonization and get these kids back in touch with their roots. When they come out of it, often something has changed deep within them, and some of these gang members become beautiful human beings. It's important never to give up. Some of the kids I work with do terrible things. Some of them are sitting in prison. But we don't give up on them.

DJ: It sounds as if you're saying that one of the most important things we can do, not only to help get kids out of gangs, but also to undermine capitalism, is to value children for who they are.

LR: Valuing children sounds so innocent, but if we really put it into practice, it would destroy capitalism. Capitalism cannot withstand that kind of change in values. If you start bringing forward these communal, traditional, cooperative ways of living—which are far older than capitalism—capitalism will begin to wither. Capitalism is based on scarcity, whereas these traditions are based on abundance.

In the temporary communities we create with these kids, we try to give them the knowledge, love, and attention they need to go forward on their own paths and become responsible for their own journeys. Capitalism tries to force us into the molds of factory worker, manager, and so on, instead of recognizing that each of us is imprinted with some destiny that we have to fulfill, some place we must go, regardless of race or class.

And once you've gone out into the world and found your own destiny, you have to come back and use your new understanding to strengthen your community. It isn't like the American Dream, where you go to college, get a well-paying job, and leave behind forever the town where you grew up. Your community owed it to you to help you find your potential, and you owe it to your community to give back more than it gave to you.

When I was growing up, I took so much away from my community. I hurt a lot of people. I may not be spending my life in prison, like some guys I knew growing up, but that's just because I got away with my crimes. I took from my community, and now I need to give back to it. So I've sentenced myself to a lifetime of community service. No judge made me do this. I do it because it's what I need to do. And I serve through my writing, my words, my work—not through something outside of myself.

DJ: Through the center of your being; just through who you are.

LR: To me, this is where the real revolution lies. Because revolution is a healing process. There's a wound in the land, in the center of the culture, in all of us, and we need to take a healing road. We need to heal personally, communally, and socially, and to participate in the healing of the land. Revolution should be a kind of rebalancing, not just an attempt to overturn the government and get rid of the people who run it.

DJ: Where do drugs fit into all of this?

LR: Drug culture is American culture. The situation has changed dramatically over the past thirty years. The kids who were using heavy drugs like heroin when I was a kid were poor Mexicans—in other words, only the marginalized kids.

Now it's not just Mexicans. Middle-class white kids are shooting up. Plus, the heroin now is many times more potent than it was thirty years ago. Back then, you had to mainline it to get a real high, and you could use it for a while before becoming addicted. Kids these days are just snorting it, and they're overdosing.

Things are starting to fall apart all over. Even the people who really believe in capitalism, who benefit the most from it, are dying from it, too. Capitalism is killing middle-class white children as well as the poor. Those weren't gang members who carried out the Columbine killings. Those were middle-class kids. You know which community has the highest number of heroin addicts per capita in the country? Plano, Texas—a gated community. What do you do when even living in a gated community isn't going to save you? There's a great street saying: what goes around comes around. You can't kill off the Indians and rob them of their land and build an industrial society that steals the blood and soul of every immigrant and not pay a price for it. We've all paid a tremendous price for it, and we'll continue to pay.

Heroin addiction, alcoholism, and gangs are just symptoms of much deeper problems. And one of those problems is that we no longer have anything resembling a spiritually-based communal life. I took drugs for seven years, and then I drank for twenty years. Now I've been sober for six. But for that twenty-seven years, I was sleepwalking, not believing in anything.

DJ: How did you get sober?

LR: It began with writing *Always Running*. Finally telling that story after twenty-some years was extremely healing. And I had to do it. My son Ramiro was in a gang, and I wanted to save him, but I felt totally inadequate. I didn't know what it meant to be his father. I didn't know what to do. So I wrote that story for him.

The process of opening up to all the terrible things I'd done was transformative. But I was still drinking, and my drinking was taking me away from my kids, my writing, my marriage, everything. I couldn't go to AA. I'd tried it three times.

I knew a lot of people whose lives had changed because of AA, but I knew myself well enough to see that I would have become addicted to it. Drugs and alcohol are all-consuming, but so is recovering from them. I didn't want to be consumed by either. I went through a Rational Recovery program, a non-twelve-step alternative to AA. The program made it clear that if I was rationalizing drinking, I could just as well rationalize not drinking. I started putting my life together, and pretty soon I didn't want to drink anymore.

I won't lie to you: heroin feels good. You can't tell kids, "Just say no." It's a great feeling. In order to let it go, you've got to have something better to replace it. One of the reasons so many poor kids—and now rich kids—do heroin is that it's one pleasure society can't take away. Cops and teachers and other adults may look down on you, but none of them can deny you that pleasure. The physical addiction is strong, but nowhere near as strong as your brain's grip on that lonely pleasure.

DJ: It's that spiderweb again.

LR: Exactly. Your brain has to change its viewpoint, change its vision, and stop holding on to that pleasure. Only then can you say, "I'm never going to do drugs or alcohol again." That's the only way to get off it and stay off it.

DJ: What's the relationship between sobriety and revolution?

LR: There's a strong connection, because drugs are one way people avoid vital issues in their lives. Drugs take everything away, leaving you with no time for anything else, whether it's raising a family, getting a decent job, understanding yourself, or trying to transform the world.

I've been a revolutionary for a long time, but after I became sober, I realized how inadequate all my previous efforts had been, because so much of my energy had gone into finding my next drink. It was the one need that came before all others. When I was able to get drinking out of the way, I began learning more, reading more, writing more, and meeting more people. I began trying to communicate more with my own kids, and also with kids in the community. I started my own press, Tia Chucha Press, named after my favorite aunt. I helped create Youth Struggling for Survival here in Chicago and cofounded a group called Rock A Mole in Los Angeles that puts together music and art festivals. I couldn't have done any of this when I was drinking.

DJ: It seems to me that one of the most important things we can do to change this culture is to create alliances between groups with common interests, like farmers and environmentalists. How can we do that with inner-city kids?

LR: Someone once pointed out to me that the word *respect* comes from the Latin *respectus*, which means "to see again." It's a beautiful concept. We have to see each other again. We have to see the gang member again, and the poor farmer, too. As we see them again, we find they're not that different from us, that a thread connects us all: the Indian on the reservation and the immigrant just arriving on these shores; the middle-class kid in the suburbs and the gang member in the inner city. The more we look, the thicker that thread becomes. Sometimes it may be invisible, but it's there. We've got to make it more visible. There is no such thing as a separate reality. What we do here affects people over there.

DJ: What you're saying is doubly true for two kids from different parts of the ghetto, wearing different-colored shirts.

LR: That's what I try to get these gang members to realize: that a kid from another gang is a human being just like them. I tell them to ask themselves why they want to kill this other person. What is the history behind it—not just the recent history of "He beat up one of my friends," but the larger history? How much of their anger is real, and how much of it is the result of manipulation, or of not seeing clearly?

DJ: Does what you're saying apply also to the cops who are beating these kids up or manipulating them into killing each other?

LR: That's an important and difficult question, and leads to one of the most difficult questions of all: that of violence.

I won't say whether violence is or isn't necessary, but I do think most revolution is nonviolent. Most of what we're talking about is teaching and healing. I think a lot about the Zapatistas in Mexico. They came down from the mountains with guns when they started, but most of their fighting has been through poetry and words. It's important to note, however, that the Zapatistas do carry guns. They haven't walked down like lambs to the slaughter. So I can't say we should never be armed. But it must be done in connection with larger issues. The beauty of the Zapatistas, or of others like them, is that they know there's something bigger empowering them. It has to do with the imagination, with reexamining our ideas and perceptions and laying bare the basics of who we are.

If I look at a cop and see him as just a man in a uniform, he's my enemy. But if I could see him at home trying to raise his family, then I could see he's just like me. It's what his badge represents that I want—and need—to deal with, not the cop, who's just a fellow human being, no better or worse than you or me. I want to destroy the system that put that cop in a position where he can beat up me or my kid, where he can come into my house and decide what is right and wrong. But I have absolutely no desire to kill that particular person, who may have to do whatever it is he's doing just to make a living.

It's extremely important for us to examine the issue of violence, because it isn't theoretical. Violence is a given in our society. Some of these kids are armed to the teeth. I always tell gang members, "If you're going to die for a five-block piece of land that you don't even own, or for the name of a gang, or for someone's shoes or jacket, you're selling your life very cheap. If you're going to die for something—and we all die someday, anyway—why not die for something big? Die for the whole world."

Of course, we need to move the emphasis away from dying. When I was a kid I would ask myself what I was willing to die for. Now I ask what I'm willing to live for. And if you know what you want to live for, you begin to want to live; you do everything you can to live. And you no longer want to kill, because part of the reason people want to kill is that they don't care if they die.

In my talks, I get really adamant about the need for change, and once somebody asked me, "Are you talking about overthrowing the government?"

I said, "No, I'm talking about overthrowing the consensus that we all participate in that allows kids to be killed in the street." That's what I'd like to see overturned. The governmental and economic systems couldn't exist in a society where we took care of everyone, a society with no poverty, no homelessness, nobody hungry, nobody needing medical care and dying just before they get to the steps of the hospital because they don't have insurance.

Things can change, even in a cynical world where so many perceptions are deeply entrenched. We must undermine the idea that the current system is somehow inevitable and immutable. One place we see this idea enshrined is in prison. Sadly, I know about that.

My son is serving a twenty-eight-year sentence in a maximum-security prison. I go to see him as often as I can. He tries to keep his spirits up, but recently he said, "I can't see myself changing. I can't see myself losing this rage." I know he was just repeating what everything in his surroundings tells him. He was buying into what the system wants him to believe: that he'll always be crazy. But my own experience is proof that change is possible. I'm very gentle now. Not that long ago, you wouldn't have wanted to get near me. And if I can change, then anyone can.

The belief that things can't change is central to the logic of addiction. When you're surrounded by pathology and abuse, it's easy to feel you can never break free of that web. Nobody says change is easy. It takes effort. But it's possible. That's why I called one of my books *It Doesn't Have to Be This Way*. When you're in a gang, you feel you'll never leave it. Gang members often say, "Can't stop, won't stop." But then they learn some small lesson or discover a different way of looking at things, and suddenly the world cracks open for them, and they see that it doesn't have to be this way. We don't have to live in a world where more poor kids go to prison than to college.

If we really want revolutionary change, if we really want kids to stop killing and dying in the streets, we need to reimagine society. For me, it all starts with saving these kids. We have to have courage and put our morality on the line. We can talk about morality all we want, but it really boils down to this: when my neighbor's house is burning, am I going to jump in and save him? His life versus mine. That's the true test of it. And right now the house is burning around these kids, and the most moral people I know are the few who are diving in to save them—and, in the process, saving themselves.

RICHARD DRINNON

Interview conducted at
his home in Port Oxford, Oregon,
December 11, 1998.

Richard Drinnon grew up in the Pacific Northwest, surrounded by the region's lush forests and rivers dense with fish and waterfowl. Within his lifetime, it has all been lost to industrialization. The salmon are gone, as are the geese. The Columbia River has been turned into a "cement sluice, a ditch," decimated. Salmon: gone. Geese: gone. River: gone. He also had friends in high school who were hauled off to internment camps. Japanese-Americans: gone.

By his reckoning, these atrocities spring from this culture's same cultural imperative: the need to dominate wild nature and any humans guilty by association. That especially includes the indigenous, who make their homes with the land, in a "symbiotic relationship." As Drinnon points out, "Respect for land makes respect for self and others possible." And the opposite has come true again and again across the history of Western expansion around the globe: the European imperative to dominate the land creates "a bone-certainty . . . that we must" commit genocide against the people who are part of the land.

Through five books and across as many decades, Drinnon has explored the grim metaphysics of the necessary relationship between civilization, racism, hatred, and land theft. His book *Facing West: The Metaphysics of Indian-Hating and Empire-Building* (University of Oklahoma Press, 1997) was a National Book Award finalist. His book about Japanese-American internment camps, *Keeper of Concentration Camps: Dillon S. Myer and American Racism* (University of California Press, 1987) was described as "riveting" by the *New York Times*. Drinnon is also the author of *Rebel in Paradise*, a biography of Emma Goldman, as well as *White Savage: The Case of John Dunn Hunter*. His work has appeared in the *Massachusetts Review*, the *Nation*, and numerous other journals. Drinnon received his PhD from the University of Minnesota and is professor emeritus of history at Bucknell University. He lives in Coos Bay, Oregon.

Derrick Jensen: In your book *Facing West: The Metaphysics of Indian-Hating and Empire-Building*, you quote a turn-of-the-century U.S. military officer in the Philippines: "We exterminated the American Indians, and I guess most of us are proud of it, or, at least, believe the end justified the means; and we must have no scruples about exterminating this other race standing in the way of progress and enlightenment, if it is necessary."

Richard Drinnon: That quotation goes to the heart of a continuity in American history that extends from the earliest settlements across the continent, into the Pacific, and beyond. Too many historians place emphasis on differences among specific events. This makes it more difficult to see patterns. Instead of analyzing the massacre of the Pequots, or the massacres at Wounded Knee or My Lai, we should talk about the thread that connects them all.

DJ: What is that thread?

RD: It's the assumption that there is only one way to understand reality, and that the carriers of Western Civilization—the English, and from them the Americans—are the sole possessors of that one way, and that their mission is to spread light and Civilization wherever they go. Those who don't understand the world in the one "correct" way are expendable. Sometimes, as in the case of African slaves, they are considered useful, but if their usefulness comes to an end, then they, too, are dispensed with.

Racism is central to this mindset. A central theme of American history is a conviction that nonwhites are human only under certain circumstances, and then only by way of toleration. There is a line running from the seventeenth century settlements along the Atlantic seaboard, from the massacre of the Pequots (although one could just as easily start at Jamestown or any other early colony), to a few months ago, when President Clinton showed himself ready to distract attention from his difficulties by sending Tomahawk missiles to destroy a pharmaceutical factory in the Sudan. It makes a huge difference that the Sudanese are African, and are thus not as fully human as somebody in France, Britain, or Germany. It makes a difference that our leading enemy of the moment, who has no means of delivering his Tomahawks to our physical presence, is a Saudi Arabian, Osama bin Laden, a strange figure with a strange name, and most important of all, a dark face.

That officer in the Philippines I quoted was merely being perceptive, more perceptive than most of us like to be when we think about our history.

DJ: Who is it okay to kill?

RD: Well, it's okay to kill the night watchman at the Al Shifa factory in Sudan. It's okay to kill people in camps in Afghanistan. It was okay to kill 150,000 Iraqis in 1991, during the so-called Gulf War. And now it's okay for us not to get too concerned that in the eight years since Operation Desert Storm, sanctions have killed perhaps five million Iraqis.

Someone pointed out to our Secretary of State, Madeline Albright, that about five hundred thousand children have been killed by the sanctions, then asked, "Is the price worth it?"

Albright replied, "We think the price is worth it." This response is the kind of quick writing off of people that happened in Vietnam, and before that in the Philippines, and before that in the genocidal destruction of the Indians in California, and before that . . . We can work our way back across the country and back through time and see those in power delivering precisely the same sentiments in essentially the same words.

DJ: Why is it okay to kill these others, whether they are Pequots or California Indians?

RD: Or Filipinos, or Vietnamese, or Iraqis. Why is it? On one level, it's not okay. We don't normally turn to each other and say, "Yes, it's okay to kill any number of nonwhites."

DJ: Although just last weekend I played basketball against a guy wearing a shirt that said, "I'd fly 1,000 miles to smoke a camel jockey."

RD: And I'm sure you've seen the bumper stickers that read: "Save a fish, spear an Indian."

But the racism is not normally so overt. That kind of open expression isn't so often advanced by a spokesperson for the State Department, or by somebody giving a backgrounder at the Pentagon. But whether the expression is evident or hidden, the underlying assumption remains, which is that it's much easier and more desirable to have a nonwhite enemy than, say, a German enemy.

That doesn't mean whites never kill other whites. We did indeed bomb Germany in World War II, but we never developed toward the Germans the same kind of mercilessness we developed toward the Japanese. John W. Dower, in his good book *War Without Mercy*, shows that our demonization of the Japanese far exceeded that of the Germans. I recall this from my own experience watching propaganda films in the Navy Air Corps. The Germans were sort of misguided. If they could only get rid of Hitler and his gang we could bring them around. Kind of a quarrel in the family. The Japanese? No.

This is evident in how we treated Japanese-Americans. At Tule Lake, in California, just a couple of hundred miles from where we are now, there was a German prisoner of war camp and a Japanese-American concentration camp. The Germans, who of course were not American citizens, were allowed out of the camp. They could bicycle into town. But the Japanese-Americans, many of whom were American citizens, were kept behind barbed wire. At the same time, German and Italian nationals who lived in the United States—even those who were avid supporters of Hitler or Mussolini—were not picked up. Imagine the outcry if Vince and Dom and Joe DiMaggio had been placed in concentration camps based solely on their Italian heritage! Yet most people didn't disapprove when it came to these "others," the Japanese. Fears of the "yellow peril" ran up and down the West Coast. When I was in high school in Salem, Oregon, I had some second generation Japanese-American (Nisei) friends, yet it didn't seem unfair to me that after Pearl Harbor these friends of mine were hauled off to horse stalls at the fairgrounds. The racism is embedded that close to home, and that deeply.

DJ: Isn't some form of xenophobia inherent in all of us? I think of Indian groups whose name for themselves is "The People," implying that everyone else is not "the people."

RD: The name strikes you and me as xenophobic since a cardinal principle of our Western Civilization has been what one anthropologist calls "the negation of the other." By contrast tribal cultures affirmed "the other who affirms you," and this principle of affirmation always carried with it the possibility of extending "the people" outward, beyond family and clan and tribe to all other beings and things in a universal embrace—adoption!—that would reflect the very antithesis of xenophobia, or, as I once ventured, "humankind's unconscious yearnings for the unity of all people and lands."

For those of us of European background, the principle of negation of the other has traditional ties to skin color. Over the centuries our reactions to degrees of melanin pigment in the skin and other identifiable hereditary characteristics have differentiated this racism from xenophobia and ethnocentrism and buried it far more deeply and explosively within the Western psyche.

Here a homey illustration from a current biography may help. Houston native Barbara Jordan was born black, too black. "Why is she so dark?" her father immediately asked, fully anticipating how hard it would be for her to compensate for her crippling color. To become the first African-American woman ever elected to Congress from the South, she had to leap two barriers, one imposed by white hatred and the other by a carbon-copy black prejudice against her darkness. The two barriers merged in a black-is-ugly aesthetic that made ethnocentrism seem almost benign in comparison.

Contrast that to the British, who, for all their trying, have never really been able to make the Irish into "black" figures. They called them Black Irish and tried their damnedest to make them into "white niggers," but that oxymoron wouldn't wash in racist parlance, suggesting the term is too irrational even for something—racism—that is by definition irrational.

The distinction between who are the victimizers and who are the victims— that is, who should fall naturally into the role of master and who should fall just as naturally into hauling water and hewing wood—has been made primarily on the difference of complexion, shading off into culture, language, and the like. Some historians try to make the case that the first blacks the Europeans brought to this continent in the 1600s had it no worse than white indentured servants, but I don't think that's supportable. Most of the indentured servants were enslaved for a specific period of time, while most Africans were released only by death. They were commodities. Intermarriage was disallowed by statute.

We can follow the racism further back, across the Atlantic. We know that before John Smith came to America, he served in Africa, and so had prior experience dealing with what the English used to call "the lesser breeds." We know that the Spanish and Portuguese had a considerable jump on the British so far as colonizing Africa and enslaving Africans. We can take it even further back than this. We know that when the Roma, or Gypsies, started moving into Europe about 1000 CE, the Europeans responded to them as vermin, vile, brown creatures. The Gypsy hunts in Europe presaged Indian hunts that took place later in America and Aborigine hunts in Tasmania. The response to these nonwhite outsiders was, and in many ways continues to be, similar to the response of white Europeans to other peoples they have encountered in the great eruption of Europe into the rest of the world.

The rationalizations for this racism have always kept pace with the times. In the nineteenth century, we had the scientific explosion surrounding the Darwinian notion of natural selection. This led inevitably to an explosion of scientific racism, which declared that nonwhites were genetically inferior and thus destined to be superseded by whites. Along these lines, Darwin noted that soon "the civilised races of man will almost certainly exterminate, and replace, the savage races throughout the world." Natural selection became the explicit justification for racism, and joined religion in furthering exploitation and genocide.

DJ: What is the fundamental difference that racist whites perceive in their own minds between themselves and those they consider "the lesser breeds"?

RD: Again, this can be traced back to Europeans' early encounters with non-whites. Apart from skin color, the difference was seen to be between those who could think, those who could plan, those who could control and dominate; and those who could not. Because blacks and Indians were viewed as children, or beasts, it was believed they could not control themselves, and so needed to be controlled. We can follow this thread back to the Age of Reason, where those in power came up with ways to distinguish those who possessed reason from those who were creatures of their bodies, of the flesh.

DJ: The notion of "those who could reason" versus "those who could not" goes back even further. The word *barbarian* came from the Greek name for their uncivilized neighbors, who, according to the Greeks, spoke only gibberish: bababa. And then there's the Bible, with the Chosen People exterminating the unchosen ones living in the Promised Land. Put that alongside your quote from the officer in the Philippines, and there's your continuity.

Which brings me to another question. Do you think we destroy these others because we want their land, or do you think we want their land because we hate and want to destroy them? Or do you think it is some combination?

RD: I see it as a combination. Sure, part of it is simple economics: we want what they've got. We see them running through the trees, and we perceive the trees as so many thousands of board feet which can be converted to so many dollars, so it doesn't take us long to convince ourselves that these forest-dwelling people need to be removed to the desert. When we later discover uranium under the desert, well, we need to kick them off again. All the fine words several hundred years ago about Christianizing the natives, and all the fine words today about "the free market," are simply cloaks for the same old drive to get Indian land and resources.

But economics doesn't account for it all. In order for us not only to take their land but feel good about doing it, we must perceive the land as empty. By far the dominant American fantasy has been that of an open continent, of unoccupied territory, not only terra incognita, but also terra vacuus—empty. Americans are not the only ones to share this fantasy. It contributed to Hitler's lebensraum policy, which he explicitly stated was based on the Manifest Destiny policy of white Americans, and certainly it is shared by mainstream Israelis, with the assumption from Ben-Gurion on down that Palestinians really don't exist in any full sense.

But there's still a missing piece. Economics and feeling good about ourselves cannot account for the implacable hatred, and for the glee in destruction we have so often seen. Describing the slaughter of the Pequots, one old soldier reminisced that the killers were like men in a dream: "then was our Mouth filled with Laughter, and our Tongues with Singing." This too is part of the pattern that wends its way down to today. Why? The missing piece seems to be that of dominion over nature. We—Europeans, descendants of Europeans, Civilized peoples—need to have dominion over what is "out there." These other people are in what is "out there," which means they must be dominated. These are deeply held convictions, not just rationalizations dreamed up to facilitate economic exploitation. This is an imperative that creates a bone-certainty among those committing genocide that we not only have the right to destroy these others, but that we must.

In the end our attempts to dominate nature will cause us to catch ourselves in the same trap we've set for all the others. Even the dominators are a part of nature, which means that those who set out to dominate nature must ultimately dominate themselves. Dominating ourselves means we're going to live in ways we don't want to live, express things we don't want to express, and find things out about ourselves we don't want to find out.

DJ: It seems pretty clear that an urge to destroy underlies many of our activities. I wonder how much of that urge is based on a need to eradicate those who represent other ways to be, and who thus remind us of what we're losing. You cite Increase Mather as saying, "People are ready to run wild into the woods again and to be as Heathenish as ever if you do not prevent it."

RD: There had to be strict laws in the New England colonies against fraternization with Indians, because so many Saints were so willing to throw off their Sainthood and live in the forest with the forest-dwellers, to throw off their rigid embrace of Puritanism and to embrace instead their bodies, to dance, as is so important to Indians, and to fall into relatedness, to allow themselves to be possessed by this shaggy New World instead of being mere possessors of it.

We are of our bodies, and we cannot too long deny it. Our body always comes back to haunt us, to tempt us. And so it and all who remind us of it must be destroyed. This is of course one reason for the widespread misogyny within our culture. Men will say, she can bear children and I can't. But I can bear splendid theories, and in an attempt to define myself independently, I must declare she cannot. And if she can give life, surely I can take it. Which of us then is the more potent?

Lurking in the deepest recesses of European and by extension American experience is the assumption that those who are closest to the body, those who run wild through the woods, those who aren't shut up, those who haven't denied themselves and channeled their energy into something else, into building an estate, into building a city on the hill, as one of our Puritan forefathers put it, must be tamed. And we will not rest, for truly we cannot, until they are.

DJ: I'm thinking about the constant references on the part of Europeans to tribal peoples the world over as "lazy." There's a great line written by a Danish traveler after he went to what is now South Africa; he said that the Khoikhoi, a group of people we've since eradicated, "find it strange that we, the Christians, work, and they say that we are all mortal, that we gain nothing from our toil, but at the end are thrown underground, so that all we have done is in vain."

RD: We can easily turn all the accusations of sloth on their head by arguing that happy, contented people, or those who have some sense of themselves, and who they are, and where they are, don't constantly want to transcend themselves and instead simply stay more or less where they are, and not feel as though they have to go out as projectiles to conquer the rest of the world.

Frederick Turner, in *Beyond Geography*, argued that Western Civilization has expanded as a wave of dissatisfaction spreading from a core. Now there are more and more peoples who have been moved by us to become dissatisfied, who have gained the urge to go beyond their own geography, to go beyond who they are.

A sense of place is critical. For people who live with the land, the land becomes the center of their universe. It's a marriage. We are meant to be in a symbiotic relationship with the land where we live, and the notion that this relationship should be transcended is central to many of our problems, and to many of the problems we've created for others. Land is something to be respected, and this respect for land makes respect for self and others possible.

When I taught in Pennsylvania I used to take my students to open pit mines. Some of the most effective teaching I ever did consisted of nothing more than sitting on the edge of these five-story-deep holes, looking across at a town under which fires still burned. Smoke still came up in the streets.

What we do to the land says much about who we are. All I have to do is go back up the country road here two or three miles to see an area that is clearcut, that is virtually destroyed. I wish readers of the interview could see what's been done up there. One look at a clearcut is more compelling than any number of words.

DJ: Let's talk about respecting the land. You spoke a while ago of dance being important to Indians. In *Facing West* you quote Johan Huizinga, who said, "The concept of play merges quite naturally with that of holiness. Any Prelude of Bach, any line of tragedy proves it. . . . Primitive or . . . archaic ritual is thus sacred play, indispensable for the well-being of the community, fecund of cosmic insight and social development." He also called Indian dances "pure play . . . The purest and most perfect form of play that exists."

RD: I'm not much of a dancer, but as I began working with this material, dancing forced itself on my attention. I found that the more I read and tried to understand, the more it became clear that the white settlers really disliked the fact that Indian kids weren't whipped into line, really didn't like the absence of discipline, really didn't like the way these others loved to dance. This dancing, this showing of their "bronzed thighs and shoulders," was, to the minds of the settlers, devil worship.

Dance was and is worship, but not of the devil. In dance the Indians express their relatedness to the land and to each other. Sioux Chief Standing Bear said of the Indian that "All the joys and exaltations of life, all his gratefulness and thankfulness, all his acknowledgments of the mysterious power that guided life, and all his aspirations for a better life, culminated in one great dance—the Sun Dance." If you do not look on the body as fallen, dance may be a celebration of creation, and of the flesh.

DJ: I never liked dancing at all, until one day I went to an Indian Pow Wow. There I became entranced by the dances, and said to the person next to me, "I could see myself doing that." Of course I could safely say that, knowing I would never dance because of the question of cultural appropriation. But then the announcer said the next dance, called a friendship dance, was open to everyone, including whites. I'd put my foot in it and so had no choice but to participate. It was wonderful. I loved it.

RD: A group called White Roots of Peace used to come by the school where I taught in Pennsylvania. The group was made up mainly of Mohawks. They insisted that those in the audience participate in their dance. It was beautiful. Dancing is not something to be relegated to a ballroom.

DJ: Or a bar. Bill McKibben has a great essay about how so much of our dancing has to do with shaking our booties, in essence with sublimated sex. Sex may be a fine thing to dance about, but why is it the only thing? What about the harvest? What about community? What about the river or the trees? What about dances simply of joy?

RD: I'm sure you know the work of the Spokane Indian Sherman Alexie. In an article about the opening of a movie based on one of his books, he's quoted as saying, "Indians are the most joyous people in the world. The two funniest groups of people I've been around have been Indians and Jews. So I guess there's something to be said about the inherent humor of genocide." Isn't that nice? Even after two hundred years of oppression, ever since Lewis and Clark entered the region, he can still find humor there. I'm certain this has to do with his attention to the dance (and in his case, probably basketball), to this kind of sacred play.

DJ: You also wrote a biography of Emma Goldman. Everything we're talking about seems to relate to a phrase that was very important to her: "Wenn Du es nicht fühlst, wirst Du es nicht erraten"—If you do not feel a thing, you will never guess its meaning.

RD: When I began that book I was essentially a socialist, and as with dance, the more I got into the book, the more my perspective opened up. Although Emma Goldman had been an early supporter of the so-called Russian experiment in the new Soviet Union, she quickly became disillusioned with it, and was not afraid to express this disillusionment honestly. Up till reading about that, I had been an exponent of a kind of social scientism. "Objectivity" was very important to me. But Emma Goldman helped me find my way—and any number of classes of my students would tell you, "My God, did he ever find his way!"—to be able to say to them, "We're not looking for objectivity here. We're looking for honesty." As much of it as we can come by.

And this honesty isn't a problem when it comes to something we don't give a shit about. If I don't care for something, there is no problem with me telling you the truth. But if I do care, and there exists some evidence that makes my position awkward, it becomes a bit more tempting to try to cover it up or distract attention away from it. But that's no way to have discourse, and it's no way to live.

If you don't feel a thing, you'll never guess its meaning. That is the opposite of where we are. Where can an attempted dominion over nature and self lead but to the eradication of feelings in any kind of fully human way? Where can it lead but to a mindset that creates people who can say, "Five hundred thousand Iraqi children is a price we can afford to pay"? We can kill, but can we feel?

DJ: Emma Goldman said that one of the most influential books she ever read was a novel entitled *What Is to Be Done?*

RD: That's the question, isn't it? Considering the insistence with which those who dominate have gone about their business, I am continually amazed at those who continue to resist. Think about the Indians. For generations they've been killed or kicked off their land, their children were sent away to boarding schools, they were told they couldn't speak their own languages, and they were forbidden from dancing. All kinds attempts were made to erase their memory of who they were and where they came from. And that has transformed them. R.D. Laing was right when he wrote that if you destroy a people's experience their behavior will be destructive. There is no better way to understand alcoholism or suicide among Indians. Despair. The experience of being destroyed.

Yet some continue to resist. When I get too pessimistic I always think about those who resist, and about those who continue to say, "There is fun. There is pleasure to be had here." Not the lightweights who would have us ignore the great sorrow and despair, but those who can pass through it, who can experience the despair yet still find joy in living. For life really is wonderful.

Like our bodies, these cultures are resilient. We have taken their land and driven roads through the center of their universe. If it were me, I think I would feel as though it had been driven through my heart. Yet they persevere. Their cultures go underground and take shapes that are harder to see. I take heart from their continued existence. I take heart from the fact that many of the Africans who were brought here as slaves survived, and they came up with the blues, and jazz, and other treasures.

What is to be done? I think often we constrain ourselves to "feel-good" messages, where the endings are always happy, the difficulties easily surmountable. But those messages go nowhere, they don't even comfort us, and are almost impossible to maintain against the evidence of our own senses. Much better, I believe, and more honest, is to look our despair in the eye and be heartened by an ongoing resistance that is our last best hope, however forlorn that hope sometimes seems.

Growing up in the 1930s, I used to hitchhike with a friend up the Willamette Valley to Vancouver, Washington, and then hop freight trains up the Columbia River to Pasco. We would thin apricots in Yakima, or work the pea harvest in Milton-Freewater, or work in a cannery down toward Pendleton. Riding the rails up the Columbia Gorge was one of the most memorable experiences of my life. All the ducks and geese. The river.

Recently I took our daughter and son-in-law along the same route—by car this time—and I couldn't recognize it. The Columbia has become a cement sluice. A ditch. The Bonneville Dam was just going in when I was a kid. Now there are many dams. Just within my lifetime the Columbia has been lost. Now the salmon, huge runs of salmon, can't get up the Snake. They're gone.

The same is true of San Francisco Bay. When I taught at Berkeley in the late 1950s and early 1960s, I belonged to an organization called Save the Bay. Now the Bay is contaminated with dioxin, such that people shouldn't eat the fish. We used to try to save the Bay from being filled in, but now there are places that used to be on the shore from which you can't even see the Bay. We tried our best, but it wasn't good enough. It's hard to maintain that false "feel-good" attitude in the face of this.

It may be that we have constructed for ourselves what Henry David Thoreau called an atropos, a fate. We have a system that is self-propelled, largely, by virtue of our not withholding our support from it, and not resisting it, not fighting it as hard as we can. When he wrote that, he was talking about the railroads . . .

DJ: The first of the modern corporations, by the way . . .

RD: . . . and it's a hell of a lot more of a fate now than it was then. How do you fight it?

Perhaps some of it has to do with timing. In the 1950s I argued that we should look upon politics as a form of tragedy. One of the leading heroes I had at the time was a young woman from Hungary who threw herself under the treads of an invading Russian tank. I thought that with the system we've got, maybe it isn't possible for human beings to live decently unless they throw themselves under the tracks. But that was overwrought, and too accepting of the situation, because the situation was changing even then.

In 1956, Rosa Parks had already refused to move to the back of the bus, her refusal being part of an ongoing campaign. Montgomery, Alabama, was set to move, and out of that was to come Martin Luther King, Jr. and all of the others. At the time, I was teaching American history, and American history was spinning out of control. It can happen again.

DJ: The psychologist Rollo May wonderfully retold the story of Briar Rose, modifying the emphasis; no longer is she a mere sleeping beauty waiting to be awakened by a kiss, but instead she runs the story. More important than the kiss is the unconscious process of maturation she undergoes while sleeping. It is now she who determines when she will be awakened.

RD: One of the reasons for the success of the antiwar movement in the 1960s was that we were able to put a million people in Washington, and clog things up. We had days and nights of resistance, and by 1970 were able to go a fair way toward slowing down what was going on inside the Beltway.

We were taken more seriously then than now, in part because we had a politics of the streets, in which people literally took to the streets. We didn't simply march down obediently on some November day to make our little marks in their boxes. We faced problems down on our own terms. We aren't doing that so much now.

There was a time when the intellectual initiative was ours. During the Vietnam War we set up teach-ins, and nobody from the Department of Defense even wanted to come and present the official case, because it was so shitty. And we had Chomsky in the *New York Review of Books* talking about the responsibility of intellectuals. I think all of this needs to take place during that time of sleeping. And conversations such as this one and others that are taking place all over— in the environmental movement, the antiracist movement, the antimilitary movement, the feminist movement, movements centered around peoples of color, the indigenous resistance movement—may be part of what happens when the beauty begins to awaken.

DJ: That doesn't mean things will be easy.

RD: No, it doesn't.

DJ: The Vietnam antiwar movement, and of course the Vietnamese people themselves, may seem to have defeated the American military machine, but it's more accurate to say that the roving eye of American attention has merely shifted. Since that time the American military or its proxies have slaughtered millions of nonwhites in Angola, Guatemala, Honduras, Chile, Peru, Irian Jaya: you name it. Military budgets are as high now as they've ever been.

RD: Higher. It's important to remember that in the forty-two days of Operation Desert Storm, we dropped more bombs than did all of the Allies during World War II. On a single, small country.

DJ: It's as Herman Melville said: "Indian-hating still exists, and no doubt will continue to exist so long as Indians do." What do you do with that knowledge?

RD: I think the single most important thing any of us can do is lay bare the Indian-hating, make it known so we can deal with it. I mean this both personally—because I come out of Indian-hating circumstances . . .

DJ: We all do . . .

RD: . . . and socially. Then this awareness must move into action. We must be concerned for and stand in solidarity with the traditional Navajo and Hopi in the Four Corners Region, where shepherds are being relocated because the land is "needed" by a uranium mining corporation. We must work with the Indians opposing the nuclear waste dump in Ward Valley, or those opposing the Mt. Graham telescope, or those working to free Leonard Peltier.

I think we've got more people out there concerned about what is happening to the planet than we ever had before. In Humboldt County, California, there are a considerable number of mainly young people who have been carrying on an admirable battle against huge corporations, the Sheriff's Department, and the state and federal governments to save old growth redwoods. They may sometimes act counterproductively, but who the hell hasn't done that? At least they're involved in actions.

One of the problems we face, even in making the Indian-hating known, is that the more effectively and graphically we get our point across, the more potent and defensive is the response, and the more deeply embedded than ever is the hatred. An Indian man, Jerry Gamble, who used to be the editor of *Akwesasne Notes,* told one of my classes, "Look, all of you have got this problem, which is that you've got to face your history, but if you face your history you can't live with it. What are you going to do?"

This is a real dilemma. I used to see that all the time with my students. So many of them would march right up to the edge of a particularly difficult topic, and then they would walk away. I didn't want them to agree with any specific viewpoint; I just wanted them to confront the problem. But there were some who were able to bang their heads against the topic until they finally came to an understanding, to a response.

DJ: That reminds me of a great question asked by Ignazio Silone: "What makes a person decide whether to become an accomplice or rebel? From what source do some people derive their spontaneous intolerance of injustice, even though the injustice affects only others?"

RD: That was a question I asked in my biography of Emma Goldman. Even her sisters wanted her to shut up, but she wouldn't do it. I don't have an answer. When I was writing that book I asked a criminologist the underside of that question: how do we predict who will commit crimes of violence? He didn't know, and it became clear to me that if you can't predict that, you can't possibly hope to predict who will be able to empathize, to bring altruism to bear. To not be solely self-serving.

DJ: Ultimately it's extremely self-serving, because then we might be able to survive.

RD: To care about long-term survival is to respect what we have: this land we live on. To not care about long-term survival is to show disrespect. There is no way to show disrespect more fully than to act out the patterns we've been presented with historically.

DJ: This reminds me of one final quotation from *Facing West*, this by Lame Deer, who said that a wicasa wakan, or holy man, is one "who feels the grief of others." If we are to survive, each of us probably has to become a holy man or woman.

RD: There are seeds of this even in our own tradition. Jeremiah said, "Would that all the people of the Lord become prophets." If that happened we wouldn't have a caste of oppressors, and a caste of the exploited. It didn't happen in his time, and it won't happen in mine. I hope it happens in yours.

DJ: What gives me the most hope is that each child is a new opportunity to do things right. I love the streamer that hung above an anarchist school in Spain in the 1930s: "Children are the new world. And all dreamers are children; those who are moved by kindness and beauty. . . ."

RD: If we look and listen we have stories to guide us, stories like that of the anarchist school, like the stories of resistance, like the stories of humans living comfortably and fully on this land. These stories are to be searched for and listened to, thought over. There are stories going back to the first people on this continent, all those thousands of years when we didn't have our system of government, our jails, our chainsaws. I'm not saying these people were perfect, because they weren't. They were limited. They were not people with answers to everything. But they were human. And if we were to listen to them, to their stories, and to pay attention to their dances—and in time, join them in the dance—we might become a little more human ourselves.

JUDITH HERMAN

Interview conducted
by telephone, August 8, 1997.

When I was a child, my father beat everyone in my family but me. Because I was the youngest, he instead chose that I should watch, and listen. I remember scenes—vaguely, as from a dream or a movie of long ago—of arms flailing, or my father chasing my brother Rik around and around the house. I remember my mother pulling my father into their bedroom to absorb blows meant for her children. The rest of us sat stone-faced in the kitchen, listening to stifled groans through too-thin walls. I remember lying frozen late at night, hearing my father go into other bedrooms, and I remember waiting, watchful, till dawn, wondering when it would be my door that opened, and not another.

The worst thing my father did was not to hit us, but to deny he ever did it. Not only were bones broken, but broken also was the bedrock connection between memory and experience, between psyche and reality. His denial makes sense, not only because an admission of violence would have harmed his image as a socially respected, wealthy, deeply religious physician, but more simply because anyone who would break his child's arm would in all likelihood not be able to speak of it honestly.

We became a family of amnesiacs. There's no place in the mind to sufficiently contain these experiences, and as there was effectively no way out, it would have served no purpose for us to consciously remember the atrocities. So daily we forgot, and forgot again. There'd be a beating, followed by brief contrition, manifested by him asking, with deep emotion, "Why did you make me do it?" And then? Nothing, save the inconvenient physical evidence: the broken door, the urine-soaked underwear, the wooden room divider my brother repeatedly tore from the wall trying to pick up speed around the corner. Once these were fixed, there was nothing to remember. So we forgot, and the pattern continued. Not only battered children forget. We read in the newspaper statistics revealing that violence committed by intimate partners is this country's leading cause of injury to middle-aged women (every nine seconds a woman is beaten by her partner), and that 350,000 American children are killed or injured by their parents or guardians every year—and then we turn the page. We don't stop the horrors because we don't talk about them. We don't talk about them because we don't think about them. We don't think about them because they're too horrific to comprehend. As Judith Herman so accurately puts it, "The ordinary response to atrocities is to banish them from consciousness. Certain violations of the social compact are too terrible to utter aloud: this is the meaning of the word *unspeakable.*"

Judith Herman is one of the world's experts on the effects of psychological trauma. She received a Lifetime Achievement Award from the International Society for Traumatic Stress Studies. She is the author of *Father-Daughter Incest* and *Trauma and Recovery: The Aftermath of Violence—From Domestic Abuse to Political Terror*, a classic in the field. Not so much a self-help book as lyrically written literature, *Trauma and Recovery* is an incisive and compassionate look into the abyss of violence, and an exploration of the territory beyond. I could not stop crying when first I read the book years ago, and on reading it again more recently I once again cried, at the book's honesty, at the clarity of thought it contains, and not least, at the beauty of the book's language. I had many questions for Dr. Herman.

Derrick Jensen: What is the relationship between atrocity and silence?

Judith Herman: Atrocities are actions so horrifying they go beyond words. For people who witness or experience atrocities, there is a kind of silencing that comes from not knowing how to put these experiences into words. At the same time, atrocities are the crimes perpetrators most want to hide. This creates a powerful convergence of interest: no one wants to speak about them. No one wants to remember them. Everyone wants to pretend they didn't happen.

DJ: In *Trauma and Recovery*, you write, "In order to escape accountability the perpetrator does everything in his power to promote forgetting."

JH: This is something with which we are all familiar. It seems that the more extreme the crimes, the more dogged and determined the efforts to deny that the crimes happened. So we have, for example, almost a hundred years after the fact, an active and apparently state-sponsored effort on the part of the Turkish government to deny there was ever an Armenian genocide. We still have a whole industry of Holocaust denial. I just came back from Bosnia where, because there hasn't been an effective medium for truth-telling and for establishing a record of what happened, nationalist governmental entities are continuing to insist that ethnic cleansing didn't happen, that the various war crimes and atrocities committed in that war simply didn't occur.

DJ: How does this happen?

JH: On the most blatant level, it's a matter of denying the crimes took place. Whether it's genocide, military aggression, rape, wife beating, or child abuse, the same dynamic plays itself out, beginning with an indignant, almost rageful denial, and the suggestion that the person bringing forward the information— whether it's the victim or another informant—is lying, crazy, malicious, or has been put up to this by someone else. Then of course there are a number of fallback positions to which perpetrators can retreat if the evidence is so overwhelming and irrefutable it cannot be ignored, or rather, suppressed. This, too, is something we're familiar with, the whole raft of predictable rationalizations used to excuse everything from rape to genocide: the victim exaggerates; the victim enjoyed it; the victim provoked or otherwise brought it on herself; the victim wasn't really harmed; and even if some slight damage has been done, it's now time to forget the past and get on with our lives; in the interests of preserving peace—or in the case of domestic violence, preserving family harmony—we need to draw a veil over these matters. The incidents should never be discussed, and preferably they should be forgotten altogether.

DJ: Something I wonder, as I watch corporate spokespeople utter absurdities to defend, for example, the polluting of rivers or the poisoning of children, is whether these people believe their own claims. I'll give an example: I live less than three miles from the Spokane River, in Washington state, which begins about forty miles east of here as it flows out of Lake Coeur d'Alene. Lake Coeur d'Alene, one of the most beautiful lakes in the world, is also one of the most polluted with heavy metals. There are days when more than a million pounds of lead drains into the lake from mine tailings on the South Fork of the Coeur d'Alene River. Hundreds of migrating tundra swans die here each year from lead poisoning as they feed in contaminated wetlands. Some of the highest blood lead levels ever recorded in human beings were from children in this area. Yet just last summer the *Spokesman-Review*, the paper of record for the region, wrote that concern over this pollution is unnecessary because "there are no dead [human] bodies washing up on the river banks." To return to the original question, to what degree do both perpetrators and their apologists believe their own claims? Did my father, to provide another example, really believe his claims that he wasn't beating us?

JH: Do perpetrators believe their own lies? I have no idea, and I don't have much trust in those who claim they do. Certainly we in the mental health profession don't have a clue when it comes to what goes on in the hearts and minds of perpetrators of either political atrocities or sexual and domestic crimes. For one thing, we don't get to know them very well. They aren't interested in being studied—by and large they don't volunteer—so we study them when they're caught. But when they're caught, they tell us whatever they think we want to hear.

This leads to a couple of problems. The first is that we have to wend our way through lies and obfuscation to attempt to discover what's really going on. The second problem is even larger and more difficult. Most of the psychological literature on perpetrators is based on studies of convicted or reported offenders, which represents a very small and skewed, unrepresentative group. If you're talking about rape, for example, since the reporting rates are, by even the most generous estimates, under 20 percent, you lose 80 percent of the perpetrators off the top. Your sample is reduced further by the rates at which arrests are made, charges are filed, convictions are obtained, and so forth, which means convicted offenders represent about 1 percent of all perpetrators. Now, if your odds of being caught and convicted of rape are basically one in one hundred, you have to be extremely inept to become a convicted rapist. Thus, the folks we are normally able to study look fairly pathetic, and often have a fair amount of psychopathology and violence in their own histories. But they're not representative of your ordinary, garden-variety rapist or torturer, or the person who gets recruited to go on an ethnic cleansing spree. We don't know much about these people. The one thing victims say most often is that these people look normal, that nobody would have believed it about them. That was true even of Nazi war criminals. From a psychiatric point of view, those people didn't look particularly disturbed. In some ways that's the scariest thing of all.

DJ: Given the misogyny, genocide, and ecocide endemic in our culture, I wonder how much of that normality is only seeming.

JH: If you're part of a predatory and militaristic culture, then to behave in a predatory and exploitative way is not deviant, per se. Of course there are rules as to who, if you want to use these terms, might be a legitimate victim, a person who may be attacked with impunity. And most perpetrators are exquisitely sensitive to these rules.

DJ: To your understanding, what are the levels of rape and childhood sexual abuse in this country?

JH: The best data we have is that one of four women will be raped over a lifetime. For childhood sexual abuse I like to quote Diana Russell's data, which I believe is still the standard by which these studies are measured. She asked a random sample of nine hundred and some women to participate in a survey of crime victimization. The interviews were in-depth, and conducted in the subjects' native languages by trained interviewers. She found that 38 percent of females had a childhood experience that met the criminal code definition of sexual assault. Some people have said that because Russell's study was done in California, it's not representative, but the results from other studies have been, while slightly lower, still in the same ballpark. It's a common experience. It's less common for boys, but there is still a substantial risk for them as well.

DJ: I remember reading something like 7–10 percent.

JH: I'd say a fair estimate would be around 10 percent for boys, and two to three times that for girls. It is a little more difficult to determine levels of sexual abuse for boys, because most are victimized by male perpetrators, which adds a layer of secrecy and shame to the child's experience.

DJ: This is a huge percentage of the population that has been severely traumatized. Why isn't this front-page news every day?

JH: There is a point to be made here as well. One of the questions Diana asked her informants who disclosed childhood abuse was, what impact do you think this has had on your life? Only about one in four said it had done great or long-lasting damage. Virtually everyone said, "It was horrible at the time, and I hated it." But half of the women considered themselves to have recovered reasonably well and didn't see that it had affected their lives in a major way. I say this not to minimize the importance of what happened, but to give due respect and recognition to the resilience and resourcefulness of victims, most of whom recover without any formal intervention.

Part of the reason for this is that not all traumas are equal. Diana and I took a look at the factors that seemed to lead to long-lasting impact, and they were the kinds of things you would expect. Women who reported prolonged, repeated abuse by someone close—father, stepfather, or another member of the immediate family—abuse that was very violent, that involved a lot of bodily invasion, or that involved elements of betrayal, were the ones who had the most difficulty recovering.

You were asking why this isn't front-page news. The answer is partly that this isn't new. And it's also not something unique to this country. Wherever studies of comparable sophistication are carried out, the numbers are pretty much the same. We may have a lot more street and handgun violence than, for example, Northern Europe and Scandinavia, but private crimes are an international phenomenon.

DJ: But they aren't ubiquitous to all human cultures. I've read in multiple sources that prior to contact with our culture there have been some indigenous cultures in which rape and child abuse were rare or nonexistent. I know that the Okanagan Indians of what is now British Columbia, for example, had no word in their language for either rape or child abuse. They did have a word that meant the violation of a woman. Literally translated, it meant someone looked at me in a way I don't like.

JH: I think it would be hard to establish that rape was nonexistent in a culture. How would you determine that? But you can certainly say there is great variation. The anthropologist Peggy Reeves Sanday looked at data from over one hundred cultures as to the prevalence of rape, and divided them into high- or low-rape cultures. She found that high-rape cultures are highly militarized and sex segregated. There is a lot of difference in status between men and women. The care of children is devalued and delegated to subordinate females. She also found that the creation myths of high-rape cultures recognize only a male deity rather than a female deity or a couple. When you think about it, that is rather bizarre. It would be an understandable mistake to think women make babies all by themselves, but it's preposterous to think men do that alone. So you've got to have a fairly elaborate and counterintuitive mythmaking machine in order to fabricate a creation myth that recognizes only a male deity. There was another interesting finding, which is that high-rape cultures had recent experiences— meaning in the last few hundred years—of famine or migration. That is to say, they had not reached a stable adaptation to their ecological niche.

Sadly enough, when these risk factors are tallied, it's clear this pretty much describes our culture.

DJ: I'd like to back up for a moment to define some terms. Can you tell me more about the phenomenon of psychological trauma?

JH: Trauma occurs when people are subjected to experiences that involve extreme terror, a life threat, or exposure to grotesque violence. The essential ingredient seems to be the condition of helplessness.

In the aftermath of such experiences it is normal and predictable that traumatized people will experience particular symptoms of psychological distress. Most people experience these transiently, and recover more or less spontaneously. Others go on to have prolonged symptoms we've come to call Post-Traumatic Stress Disorder (PTSD).

It's important to note, by the way, that PTSD doesn't merely affect "helpless" women and children. We see it in combat veterans. We see it in prisoners of war. Concentration camp survivors. We see it with survivors of natural disasters, fires, and industrial and automobile accidents. We see it in cops. Sophisticated police departments now include traumatic stress debriefing for their officers involved in any sort of critical incident such as a shooting. They discovered that within two years of involvement in a critical incident, enormous numbers of well-trained, valuable, experienced police officers were being lost to disabilities, physical complaints, substance abuse, or psychiatric problems. We see it in firefighters who have to rescue people from burning buildings, and who sometimes have to bring out dead bodies. We see it in rescue workers who have to clear away bodies after a flood or earthquake. We see it most commonly in the civilian casualties, if you will, of our private war against women and children—that is, the survivors of rape and domestic violence.

DJ: What are the symptoms?

JH: It's easiest to think about symptoms in three categories. The first are called symptoms of hyperarousal. In the aftermath of a terrifying experience people see danger everywhere. They're jumpy, they startle easily, and they have a hard time sleeping. They're irritable, and more prone to anger. This seems to be a biological phenomenon, not just a psychological one.

The second thing that happens is that people relive the experience in nightmares and flashbacks. Any little reminder can set them off. For example, a

Vietnam veteran involved in helicopter combat might react years later when a news or weather helicopter flies overhead.

DJ: All through my teens and twenties when someone would ask me to go water skiing, my response externally would be to say, "No, thanks," but my internal response was, "Fuck you." I never could figure out why until a few years ago I asked my mom, and she said that there were beatings associated with water skiing trips when I was a small child. I never knew that. I just always knew that water skiing pissed me off.

JH: Sometimes people understand the trigger, but sometimes they won't have complete memory of the event. They may respond to the reminder as you did, by becoming terrified or agitated or angry.

DJ: And it doesn't have to be so dramatic as the stereotypical Vietnam vet who goes berserk when he hears a car backfire.

JH: A lot of times it's more subtle. Someone who was raped in the backseat of a car may have a lot of feelings every time she gets into a car, particularly one that resembles the one in which she was raped.

This reliving, these intrusions, are not a normal kind of remembering, where the smell of cinnamon rolls, for example, may remind you of your grandmother. Instead, people say it's like playing the same videotape over and over. It's a repetitive and often wordless reexperiencing. People remember the smells, the sounds, whether it was raining, whether it was cold. The images. Whether it was dark. Sexual abuse survivors often say, "I felt like I was smothering. I thought I was going to choke." But it's very hard for people to remember it in a kind of fluid verbal narrative that is modifiable according to the circumstances. People can't give you the short form and the long form, and describe it differently and understand it differently over time. It's just a repetitive sequence of terrifying images and sensations.

DJ: Is that symptom also physiological?

JH: Oh, yes. Studies have shown that traumatic memories are perceived and encoded in the brain differently from regular memories.

The third group of symptoms that people have—and these are almost the opposite of the intrusive nightmares and flashbacks, the dramatic symptoms—is a shutting down of feelings, a constriction of emotions, intellect, and behavior. It's characteristic of people with PTSD to oscillate between feeling overwhelmed, enraged, terrified, desperate, or in extreme grief and pain, and feeling nothing at all. People describe themselves as numb. They don't feel anything, they aren't interested in things that used to interest them, they avoid situations that might remind them of the trauma. You, for example, probably avoided water skiing in order to avoid the traumatic memories. Water skiing may not be much to give up, but sometimes people avoid relationships, or sexuality. They make their lives smaller in an attempt to stay away from the overwhelming feelings.

In addition, people with PTSD have all kinds of physical complaints. In fact, the more the culture shames people for admitting psychological weakness, the more these symptoms manifest themselves physically. Rather than seeking psychological help, people go to the doctor seeking sleeping pills, or go to the neighborhood bar to get the number one psychoactive drug available without prescription, alcohol. We see a lot of alcohol and substance abuse as a secondary complication of PTSD.

DJ: Where does dissociation fit into all this?

JH: It's central. Dissociation itself is really quite fascinating, and I don't think any of us can quite pretend to understand it. We all seem to have the capacity to dissociate, though for some people the capacity is greater. And certain circumstances seem to call it up. It involves a mental escape from experience at a time when physical escape is impossible.

When I teach, I quite often use automobile accidents to exemplify this. I'll ask people, "Can you describe what it was like in the moment before impact, the moment of impact, and the moment after?"

People often describe a sense of derealization: the thought, this isn't happening. They also describe depersonalization: this is happening, but to someone else, while I sit outside watching the crash and feeling very sorry for the person in the car. They may feel as though they're watching a movie. They describe a slowing of time. They describe a sense of tunnel vision, where they focus only on a few details, such as sounds or smells, but where context and peripheral detail fall away. Some people describe alterations of pain perception. We've all heard stories of people who walk on broken legs until they get to safety, then collapse, or people who are able to ignore their own pain while they rescue others. And then, of course, some people have amnesia. Memory gaps in the aftermath. They'll say, "I remember the moment before, and then the next thing I knew I was on the shoulder outside the car." Even with no head trauma and no loss of consciousness, there will often be a loss of memory. All of these, of course, are not specific to car wrecks, but happen with all sorts of psychological trauma.

DJ: Dissociation sounds like a very good thing.

JH: You'd think so. But more and more of the research is zeroing in on dissociation as a predictor of more long-lasting symptoms. For example, some studies were done after the San Francisco earthquake and the Oakland fire, two big disasters that happened in the last decade. Each event affected a lot of people and invoked large-scale responses by emergency personnel. Researchers interviewed and examined many survivors, then called them three, six, and more months later to see how they were doing. Well, the folks who dissociated during the earthquake turned out to be more likely to have PTSD later. There seems to be something about that altered state of consciousness that is protective at the moment, but gets you into trouble later on. People who dissociated at the time of the fire also tended to lose some of their adaptive coping in the moment. They either behaved helplessly, almost like zombies or as if they were paralyzed, or they lost the capacity to judge danger realistically. The rescue people had the most trouble with this latter group, because they would insist on going back into burning houses to rescue possessions or animals. They exposed themselves to danger, seemingly heedless of the consequences.

DJ: What's the difference between trauma and captivity?

JH: Trauma can emerge from a single event like a fire, earthquake, or auto accident, where you're in the situation, you survive it, and then you get on with your life. You may continue to relive it in fantasy, but it's not happening over and over. Even if you live in an earthquake or flood zone you still have a choice as to whether to rebuild or move away.

Based on my work with domestic abuse survivors, as well as victims of political terror, I began to ask, what happens when a person is exposed not to a single terrifying incident, but rather to prolonged, repeated trauma? I came to understand the similarities between concentration or slave labor camps or torture situations on the one hand, and on the other hand, the situation of domestic or sexual violence, where the perpetrator may beat or sexually abuse his wife or children for years on end. We see this also in the sex trade, where there's a criminally organized traffic in women and kids, and we sometimes see this sort of captivity in some religious cults, where people are not free to leave.

In situations where the trauma happens over and over, and where it is imposed by human design (as opposed to the effects of weather, or some other nonhuman force), one sees a series of personality changes in addition to simple PTSD.

People begin to lose their identity, their self-respect. They begin to lose their autonomy and independence.

Because people in captivity are most often isolated from other relationships—that this is so in normal captivity is obvious and intentional, but it is overwhelmingly the case in domestic violence as well, as perpetrators often demand their victims increasingly cut all other social ties—they are forced to depend for basic survival on the very person who is abusing them. This creates a complicated bond between the two, and it skews the victim's perception of the nature of human relationships. The situation is even worse for children raised in these circumstances, because their personality is formed in the context of an exploitative relationship, in which the overarching principles are those of coercion and control, of dominance and subordination.

Whether we are talking about adults or children, it often happens that a kind of sadistic corruption enters into the captive's emotional life. People lose their sense of faith in themselves, in other people. They come to believe or view all relationships as coercive, and come to feel that the strong rule, the strong do as they please, that the world is divided into victims, perpetrators, bystanders, and rescuers. They believe that all human relations are contaminated and corrupted, that sadism is the principle that rules all relationships.

DJ: Might makes right. "Social Darwinism." The selfish gene theory. You've just described the principles that undergird our political and economic systems.

JH: And there are other losses involved. A loss of basic trust. A loss of feeling of mutuality of relatedness. In its stead is emplaced a contempt for self and others. If you've been punished for showing autonomy, initiative, or independence, after a while you're not going to show them. In the aftermath of this kind of brutalization, victims have a great deal of difficulty taking responsibility for their lives. Often, people who try to help get frustrated because we don't understand why the victims seem so passive, seem so unable to extricate themselves or to advocate on their own behalf. They seem to behave as though they're still under the perpetrator's control, even though we think they're now free. But in some ways the perpetrator has been internalized.

Captivity also creates disturbances in intimacy, because if you view the world as a place where everyone is either a victim, a perpetrator, an indifferent or helpless bystander, or a rescuer, there's no room for relationships of mutuality, for cooperation, for responsible choices. There's no room to follow agreements through to everyone's mutual satisfaction. The whole range of cooperative relational skills, and all the emotional fulfillment that goes with them, is lost. And that's a great deal to lose.

DJ: It seems to me that part of the reason for this loss is not simply the physical trauma itself, but also the fact that the traumatizing actions can't be acknowledged.

JH: And much more broadly, because they take place within a relationship motivated by a need to dominate, and in which coercive control is the central feature.

When I teach about this, I describe the methods of coercive control perpetrators use. It turns out that violence is only one of the methods, and it's not even one of the most frequent. It doesn't have to be used all that often; it just has to be convincing. In the battered women's movement, there's a saying: "One good beating lasts a year."

DJ: What constitutes a good beating?

JH: If it's extreme enough, when the victim looks into the eyes of the perpetrator she realizes, "Oh, my God, he really could kill me."

What goes along with this violence are other methods of coercive control that have as their aim the victim's isolation, and the breakdown of the victim's resistance and spirit.

DJ: Such as?

JH: You have capricious enforcement of lots of petty rules, and you have concomitant rewards. Prisoners and hostages talk about this all the time: if you're good, maybe they'll let you take a shower, or give you something extra to eat. You have the monopolization of perception that follows from the closing off of any outside relationships or sources of information. Finally, and I think this is the thing that really breaks people's spirits, perpetrators often force victims to engage in activities that the victims find morally reprehensible or disgusting. Once you've forced a person to violate his or her moral codes, to break faith with him- or herself, you may never again even need to use threats. The fact that it's done under duress does not remove the shame or guilt of the experience. At that point the victim's self-hatred, self-loathing, and shame are so great that you don't have to beat her up, because she's going to do it herself.

DJ: That reminds me of something I read about those who collaborated with the Nazis: "A man who had knowingly compromised himself did not revolt against his masters, no matter what idea had driven him to collaboration: too many mutual skeletons in the closet. . . . There were so many proofs of the absolute obedience that could be expected of men of honor who had drifted into collaboration."

JH: Perpetrators know this. These methods are known, they're taught. Pimps teach them to one another. Torturers in the various clandestine police forces involved in state-sponsored torture teach them to each other. They're taught at taxpayer expense at our School of the Americas. The Nazi war criminals who went to Latin America passed on this knowledge. It is apparently a point of pride among many Latin American torturers that they have come up with techniques the Nazis didn't know about.

DJ: We've spent a lot of time delving into the abyss, and what I would like to do now is emerge on the other side. But first, there's something else about victims I would like to explore. You've written that symptoms of PTSD can be interpreted as a victim's attempt to tell his or her story.

JH: People not only relive the experiences in memory, but sometimes behave in ways that reenact the trauma. So a combat vet with PTSD might sign up for especially risky duty, or reenlist in the special forces. Later he may get a job in another high-risk line of work. A sexual survivor may engage in behaviors likely to result in another victimization. Especially regarding revictimization after child abuse, the data is really very sobering. One way to view this pattern is that the person is trying desperately to tell the story, in action if necessary. That's a bit teleological, but we do know that when people are finally able to put their experiences into words in a relational context, where they can be heard and understood, they often get quite a bit of relief.

DJ: You wrote in *Trauma and Recovery* that "When the truth is finally recognized, survivors can begin their recovery." How does that work? What happens inside survivors when the truth is recognized?

JH: I wish I knew. It's miraculous. I don't understand it. I just observe it, and try to facilitate it. I think it's a natural healing process that has to do with the restoration of human connection and agency. If you think of trauma as the moment when those two things are destroyed, then there is something about telling the trauma story in a place where it can be heard and acknowledged that seems to restore them. The possibility of mutuality returns. People feel better.

The most important principles for recovery are restoring power and choice or control to the person who has been victimized, and facilitating the person's reconnection with her or his natural social supports, the people who are important in that person's life. In the immediate aftermath, of course, the first step is always to reestablish some sense of safety in the survivor's life. That means getting out of physical danger, and that means also creating some sort of minimally safe social environment in which the person has people to count on, to rely on, to connect to. Nobody can recover in isolation.

It's only after safety is established that it becomes appropriate for the person to have a chance to tell the trauma story in more depth. There we run into two kinds of mistakes. One is the idea that it's not necessary to tell the story, and that the person would be much better off not talking about it.

DJ: It's over. Just get on with your life.

JH: That may work for a while, and it might be the right choice in a given circumstance, but there comes a time eventually when if the story isn't told it festers. So one mistake is suppressing it, which goes back to the silencing we spoke of earlier. These are horrible things and nobody really wants to hear or think about them. The victim doesn't, the bystander doesn't, the perpetrator certainly doesn't. So there's a very natural tendency on everyone's part to say, "Let's forget the whole thing."

The other mistake is to try to push people into talking about it prematurely, or when the circumstances aren't right, or when it isn't the person's choice. It's almost as though we respond with either numbing or intrusion. We either want to withdraw and avoid hearing the story, or we want the victim to tell all in grotesque detail. Sometimes there's a kind of a voyeuristic fascination that gets engaged. If the timing, pacing, and setting isn't right, all you're going to have is another reenactment. You're not going to have the integrative experience of putting the story into a context that makes meaning out of it and gives a sense of resolution, which is what you're really aiming for. You don't want just a simple recitation of facts, you want the person to be able to talk about how it felt, how she feels about it now, what it meant to her then, what it means to her now, how she made sense of it then, how she's trying to make sense of it now. It's in that kind of processing that people reestablish their sense of continuity with their own lives and connection with others.

DJ: This seems to be tied to mourning what was lost.

JH: Part of the motivation for the idea of "Let's not talk about it" is the belief that you can go back to the way you were before the trauma, and what people find is that's just not possible. Once you've seen, up close, the evil human beings are capable of, you're not going to see the world the same way, you're not going to see other people the same way, and you're not going to see yourself the same way. We can all fantasize about how brave or cowardly we would be in extreme situations, but people who've been exposed know what they did, and what they didn't do. And almost inevitably they failed to live up to some kind of expectation of themselves. There has to be a sense of grieving what was lost. It's only after that mourning process that people can come through it and say, "That was a hard lesson, and I wouldn't wish it on my worst enemy, but I am stronger or wiser." There is a way that people learn from adversity. People will say, "I had a crisis of faith and I found out what's important, what I really believe in."

DJ: How does an abused child mourn what he's never known?

JH: It's what you've never had that is the hardest to grieve. It's unfair. You only get one childhood, and you were cheated out of the one that every child is entitled to.

DJ: What comes next?

JH: The recovery doesn't end with the telling and hearing of the story. There is another step after that, which has to do with people reforming their connections, moving from a preoccupation with the past to feeling more hopeful for the future, feeling that they have a future, that it's not just a matter of enduring and going through life as a member of the walking dead. Instead there is an ability to knowingly affirm life even after surviving the worst other people have to dish out. And I do think that what renews people is the hope and belief that their own capacity to love has not been destroyed. When people feel damned and doomed, and feel they can't go on living, the fear often has to do with the feeling that they have been so contaminated with the perpetrator's hate, and taken so much of it into themselves, that there is nothing left but rage, hate, distrust, fear, and contempt.

When people go through mourning, and through their crisis of faith, what they come back to as bedrock is their own capacity to love. Sometimes that connection is frail and tenuous, but whether it is with animals, nature, music, or other humans, that's the bedrock to which they must return, to that one caring relationship the perpetrator was never able to destroy. Then they build from there.

As people move into their lives again, the ones who do best are the ones who've developed what Robert Jay Lifton calls a survivor mission. I've seen it happen many times. People turn their experience around and make it a gift to others. That really is the only way you can transcend an atrocity. You can't bury it. You can't make it go away. You can't dissociate it. It comes back. But you can transcend it, first by telling the truth about it, and then by using it in the service of humanity, saying, "This isn't the way we want to live. We want to live differently."

In the aftermath of terror many survivors find themselves much clearer and more daring about going after what they want in life and in relationships. They straighten things out with their families and lovers and friends, and they often say, "This is the kind of closeness I want, and this is the kind of stuff I don't want." When people are sensitized to the dynamics of exploitation, they are able to say, "I don't want this in my life." And they often become very courageous about speaking truth to power.

I have heard so many survivors say, "I know what terror is. I will live in fear every day for the rest of my life. But I also know that I will be all right, and that I feel all right." And I have heard them join others in saying, "This is the thing we want to protect, and this is the thing we want to stop. We don't know how we're going to do it, but we do know that this is what we want. And we're not indifferent." Sometimes through atrocity people discover in themselves courage that they didn't know they had.

MARC IAN BARASCH

Interview conducted
at his home in Colorado, 1999.

When Marc Ian Barasch was thirty-five years old, he had a series of vivid and startlingly detailed dreams about cancer. Though he had no physical symptoms, he went to see a doctor, insisted on medical tests, and was diagnosed with thyroid cancer. At the time, Barasch was the editor of *New Age Journal* and thought himself "quite knowledgeable about the realms of healing." But it was one thing to read and study and write about disease, and another thing to experience it.

In February 1985, he had conventional surgery. It was pronounced a success, although sorting through the spiritual, psychological, and social implications of the illness, the treatment, and its aftermath would take many years. Barasch says his life has been "affected unalterably by the singular event, both destructive and oddly ameliorative, of cancer and the titanic dreams that accompanied it." At present, he remains "vigilant about health, attentive to the inner life, and persistent in my attempts to cultivate kindness."

In part because of his long practice in Buddhism, Barasch found it essential to turn his relationship with cancer into something helpful to other people. This attitude motivated him to spend nearly fifteen years writing three books. *The Healing Path: A Soul Approach to Illness* is one of the finest books ever written about the mind-body connection. The best-selling *Remarkable Recovery* examines the commonalities among people who have spontaneously recovered from devastating illness. And *Healing Dreams* explores life-changing dreams— what Carl Jung referred to as "numinous" dreams—and their implications for understanding human nature.

One of the things I like about Marc Barasch is his refusal to abide simplistic answers. He eloquently explores the role of the spirit in disease and healing, yet also demystifies the hocus-pocus of the "If your spirit is pure, no disease can touch you" line promoted by many in the new-age movement. The relationship, he says, is far more subtle, complex, and mysterious.

The complexity of Barasch's thought is mirrored in his accomplishments. At *New Age Journal*, his emphasis on leading-edge coverage of environmental, political, and cultural issues garnered a National Magazine Award and a *Washington Monthly* award for investigative reporting. He has been a contributing editor at *Psychology Today*, editor-at-large for *Natural Health*, and has been short-listed twice for the PEN Literary Award.

Barasch was educated at Yale University, where he studied literature, psychology, anthropology, and film. A thirty-year practitioner of Tibetan Buddhism, he helped found the psychology department at Naropa University. He has worked in television and film. He is also an accomplished musician, and plays and records occasionally with a San Francisco–based "lit-rock" band that includes Stephen King, Amy Tan, and Roy Blount.

The trip to interview Marc Barasch was a return home for me. He lives just a few miles from where I grew up, in Boulder, Colorado. My first job, when I was about ten, was cleaning up the yard at a house not three blocks from his. Barasch's own yard was overgrown with bushes—or, as he put it, "allowed to flourish unhampered." When he asked me in, I wasn't surprised to find the inside of his house comfortably cluttered. He was distracted and busy—I'd caught him in the middle of a book deadline—yet nonetheless warm. As we talked, I was impressed by his intelligence. Whenever we hit upon an important point, I would see his mind leap; then he'd throw back a ladder of words so that I could follow him.

Derrick Jensen: You've written two extraordinary books about a multidimensional approach to healing, have just finished a third, and have been through the cancer mill yourself. What do you think helps people heal?

Marc Ian Barasch: I've expressed this in different ways in the different books. In *The Healing Path*, I talked about people who had gotten well against the odds. They'd done everything from chemo to carrot juice. What they had in common was that they'd all decided to look upon their disease as unique, just as they were unique, and then find a path to healing that drew upon their own enthusiasms, beliefs, and coping mechanisms. Many of them found that they went back to earlier versions of themselves, from a time before they'd gone off on a life path that had stopped making sense. In a way, it's only logical: if you treat illness as a personal journey, you're more likely to marshal your own maximum resources, both inner and outer, in addition to finding an appropriate treatment regimen. But there was also another factor: a willingness to let the illness act as a catalyst for transformation, rather than following the usual model for cure, which is an attempt to get back to the old self and the status quo.

In *Remarkable Recovery*, we researched "spontaneous remission" cases— and we did confirm that these were real cases with real medical records, many published in refereed journals. Once again, we didn't find any common method or substance that people used to heal. But we did notice what we called "congruence": a coming together of inner and outer. Independently, another researcher in Rotterdam also looking at remission cases came up with a similar description. He wrote of "a stronger congruence among emotions, cognitions, and behavior." That says to me that there must be something to it. If cancer can be understood as a form of entropy, or a growing disorder in a system, then you could say these people somehow came back into alignment with their core selves, body and soul.

Now, does this state contribute to remission, or is it just a byproduct of going through a life-changing healing journey? I don't know. These were what are called "retrospective studies." We weren't observing the ongoing process, but relying on people's subjective testimony after the fact. Still, I think the patterns are striking. If they seem inconsistent, maybe that's because the healing process took different forms according to people's personalities. It definitely wasn't a case of people becoming more serene and "spiritual." Some people got nastier, more outrageous, very emotional. Others approached things very rationally.

Our main finding was that the people who healed tended to work at getting well on all fronts. They found social support, faith, and purpose, encountered deep emotion, did things they loved, and usually chose a more healthy lifestyle, including dietary changes—though not always; one just ate greasy cheeseburgers.

DJ: I spent last evening talking to a friend's stepfather who has just been treated for cancer. Our conversation was centered around the mechanics of radiation therapy and the biochemistry of cancer. Similarly, with my own illness, Crohn's disease, I've focused most of my attention on physical causes and cures. We seem always to leave out the psyche, or the soul, in these discussions, even though doctors now concede that it plays at least some role in disease and healing. But how big a role, and of what sort?

MIB: Well, first we have to define what we mean by "soul," which is not something that flits from your body like a winged heart when you die, but rather an integrative process, an authentic way of living that embraces all our polarities—intellect and emotion, body and mind, social and private. It involves intimacy with what Taoists call "the low, the dark, and the small," and also openness to the big picture—what Zen practitioners call "big mind"—in which the ego and its needs aren't running the show. In most cultures, the soul is understood to be multiple and variegated, not some eternal, fixed, singular thing. There's an ancestral soul, a social soul, a soul that visits with the spirits.

And the soul and the imagination are intimately linked. The fact that images of the disease we are suffering—usually highly personal and fanciful images—

show up so often in our dreams suggests that illness has some business with the soul. The places where an illness deeply affects us are where we need to go to heal. Being sick batters at our emotions and has a huge existential impact. The first response—Why me?—leads straight to philosophy and religion. It affects us as social beings, in our relationships, vocation, and communities. This paradigm is as old as the biblical story of Job.

But all of these dimensions have been shunted aside in so-called scientific medicine. So many things that are considered by medicine to be "epiphenomena" or "side effects" are really central, because healing has to address the questions disease raises. It has to be a full encounter.

This is why the new approaches to illness and healing have compound names, like so-called "biopsychosocial" medicine. And this is itself an echo of earlier medical models that still exist in tribal societies, where physical illness is viewed as part of a larger constellation of imbalance—a loss of harmony with the spiritual, social, ancestral, and natural realms. Still, there's a lot of debate, especially between conventional and holistic practitioners, about just how much respective influence these different factors have.

DJ: The spiritual factor seems to be the biggest bone of contention.

MIB: And it should be, because it's so easily misunderstood. On the one hand, the effects of the mind on the body can't be refuted. We know this instinctively: when we get embarrassed, which is a purely psychosocial phenomenon, we blush, which is a purely physical function of blood flow. When we're anxious, we feel it in our stomach, and when we're in grief, we feel it in our throat; everything tightens and clenches up, and the flows of blood and neurohistamines are affected. Clearly, we're orchestrating the pharmacology of the brain through the way we perceive and react to things, through the emotional resonances of everyday events. The hormones we're marinating in cannot help but have an effect on the immune system, and thus possibly on specific disease processes, and logically on the healing process itself. It's what's generally called a "cofactor"—contributive rather than causative.

In general, the mind-body connection is not a direct causal relationship; emotion A does not create disease B. The Freudians had a field day when ulcers were thought to be caused solely by stress, but now we're finding that ulcers are more directly caused by a bacterium called campylobacter, and can be cured by a pill. On the other hand, maybe persistent anxiety creates the kind of physiological conditions in the gut that allow campylobacter to thrive. It certainly doesn't hurt ulcer patients to look at the sources of stress in their everyday lives and try to reduce them, or to go deeper into the psyche and the social environment and see what's causing all their stress. If the causes of a disease are many, then it stands to reason the disease should be treated with a multitude of approaches. We need an antidote to the old med-school dictum "One cause, one disease," which has led to the magic-bullet approach. I mean, a magic bullet can be great, but not if it means just "fixing the machine" and returning it to the way of life that made it break down in the first place.

DJ: The real trouble in this debate starts with the idea held by some that disease is a matter of "choice"—something we do to ourselves.

MIB: Yes, as if nothing just befalls us. I call it "new-age Calvinism." Calvinists, you remember, believed that if a person was prosperous, it was evidence that God loved him; and if someone was in penury, that person must be a sinner, because God, who was just and good, would never afflict a righteous person. I still see this attitude all over the place; I've even been on the receiving end of it. People have asked me, "Why do you want to have this disease?" and, "Why don't you want to get well?" and, "What spiritual ignorance is causing your illness?" No matter how fancy the wrapping on this doctrine, it too often turns into blaming the victim. I think it's a way to distance ourselves from our common fragility and impermanence, which illness shoves right in our face. In the Bible,

Job's buddy Eliphaz complains that Job's misfortunes are giving him nightmares; he's afraid maybe this mess could happen to him, too. But then Eliphaz reassures himself that Job must have done something to deserve it and says to him, rather coyly, that no one is "blameless against his Maker."

We have to be careful to try to chart a course, as psychiatrist and author David Spiegel so beautifully put it, between the "Scylla . . . [of] mindless materialism—viewing people as nothing more than the product of physical processes" and the "Charybdis . . . [of] disembodied spiritualism—the idea that if one fixes a problem in one's mind, it is fixed in the body." This whole idea of "taking personal responsibility for your disease" can get pernicious.

DJ: For a long time after I was diagnosed with Crohn's disease, all sorts of people told me, "You've got to learn to take responsibility for this." I'd like to go back and point out to them that there's a difference between being responsible for my disease, in terms of causing it, and being responsible to it, meaning being capable of responding to my body's distress.

MIB: Yes, that's it exactly. Because we do have choices in how to respond to our condition. And not just treatment choices like chemotherapy or surgery—though these can be critical—but emotional, spiritual, and social choices. With regard to the latter, for instance: do we go it alone, or join a support group? Do we reach out to friends and community, or just family? Or, looking at the psychological dimension, we might explore what Alfred Adler, Freud's breakaway disciple (he had a lot of those), called "organ dialect": what is your symptom saying—that is, what does it mean to you? How do you imagine it, dream it? How does it function in your life?

Simply examining and living with a disease can open some space for change, even if it's only a change in how we relate to it, experience it, frame it, reframe it. And this is healing, in the root meaning of that word—becoming whole; joining body, mind, and spirit. But it doesn't necessarily mean we've gotten rid of the symptom that ails us. We can be both ill and healed. We can be whole within our affliction.

DJ: I haven't heard you use the word *hope* yet. Is hope a part of the healing path? I have a friend who is HIV-positive, and soon after he was diagnosed he sent me a stack of AIDS literature. A sentence in one pamphlet grabbed me: "Eliminate false hope." What that means to me is that one shouldn't use hope as a shield against reality.

MIB: Often, hope is an extrapolation of our usual strategies projected forward into some idealized future. And maybe if we weren't so intent on this cherished fantasy, we'd find a fresh approach to illness—indeed, to life—right under our nose. Illness often means that we have to revise our expectations, let go of preconceptions.

The Buddhist ideal is to live "beyond hope and beyond fear." Many people have trouble with that. They say, "Fear's bad, sure, but hope's good; I want to hang on to that." But I've had teachers who are very ruthless on the subject. They say, "Hope and fear chase each other's tails." Either you're hoping because you're afraid of what's actually happening, or you're afraid because you worry you won't see your hopes realized. Meanwhile, that which demands your attention here and now, though it looks forbidding, may have something deeper to offer you. It's worth exploring. If hope and fear are really two sides of the same coin, then maybe you need to balance that coin on its edge.

None of this is to say that you shouldn't have a positive attitude. And there are certainly times when provisional hope—or whatever you want to call it—has been absolutely key to people's healing journeys, allowing them to take that next step and behave "as if," despite all evidence to the contrary.

DJ: When I had my worst attack of Crohn's, I was vomiting maybe twenty times a day from the pain. Had I believed I would get no better—had I not hoped the pain would subside—I might have just killed myself.

MIB: I would say that chronic disease especially requires us to exhibit a deep kindness toward ourselves. It can be important to find a way to accept our pain—accept ourselves in pain—if we can't eliminate it. I'm still haunted by a vivid dream I had when I was ill, one that seemed irritatingly irrelevant at the time, and that I just brushed aside. In it, a voice said, "The way out is the way in." That's a koan worth contemplating.

But if going in is too much for us, there's nothing wrong with stepping away. So often we're too harsh on ourselves. We expect ourselves to endure, achieve, overcome, and conquer. Being kind to ourselves in our weakness—which is really the only basis for healing—is not always the first thing we try in a crisis. Usually, we reach for the nearest blunt object and try to cudgel the problem into submission, the heroic ego to the rescue. And we usually wind up hitting ourselves in the head.

DJ: Is there a relationship between forgiveness, however you might define it, and health or disease?

MIB: I think the act of forgiveness can cut the endless cycle of action and reaction, what Buddhists would call karma. Mostly, I think forgiveness prevents you from reifying things. When you don't forgive another, you objectify that person, hardening him or her into a particular mold. In order to nurse a grudge (wonderful phrase, that, as if you must keep your grudge on life support with round-the-clock care), you always have to think of the other person as "the one who injured me." But that is only a portion of that person's being. So long as you hold on to that frozen image of the other person, the two of you will continue to play out the same dynamic. Forgiveness renders the relationship fluid again, allowing you to see other aspects of that person. And you, too, are freed to exist more fully, not frozen into one posture.

Maybe you could say the same about disease—that an unforgiving attitude reifies the disease, forcing it to hold its negative place in your personal cosmology. Then you're trapped in a fixed response, without flexibility of thought and feeling and action. But, in fact, disease and pain are never solid. The suffering is more intermittent than we think, and there can be unexpected changes. Even within the deepest pain there are moments of nonpain. In physics, light is understood to be a particle and a wave at the same time. The same is true in psychological reality.

In other words, the complexity of experience can never emerge when we're holding tightly to one particular version of it, whether we're in relationship with a person, a disease, or anything else. Of course, it's scary to enter into the no man's land of disease. We're afraid to let it speak, afraid it will swallow us up if we let it open its mouth. It's a matter of working with the shadow.

DJ: Could you define "the shadow"?

MIB: Purely psychologically—and I don't want to apply this definition to disease in general, because it's too facile—the shadow is the undeveloped and rejected parts of the self. In the course of ego development, certain things are pared away and put in the garbage heap. And they eventually start to stink. But, as with rotting vegetables or manure, there is a great fertility in this material. In a dream, for example, ugly or deformed or diseased personages may possess some disowned portion of the self. You see this in myths all the time—the troll is the keeper of the treasure, but you have to answer his riddle to get it.

Again, I don't want to romanticize illness, as if it were some wonderful path we should choose. But I have noticed that, among people who have suffered, who've had their intentions in life thwarted in some way, if they don't become embittered they usually experience soul growth, because they now know for a fact that their ego is not the supreme ruler of all things. They've transmuted suffering into humility, into humanity. The hollowing out has made them deeper, more capacious.

In dreams, this is a function of the shadow, as well. When I had cancer, believe me, I had a lot of nightmares. I could say they were all about the disease, but it's clear to me now that they were also about my spiritual and psychological blind spots. A dream can force you into the same space with the devil, this thing that is utterly repellent to you. And the dream is a closed vessel. You can't get out. So you're forced to deal with it, listen to it, try to assimilate it. And in so doing, you are transformed; you receive some of the soul moisture that, before, was locked up in ice.

Illness, obviously, is one of those things that cracks open our idealized version of the world and of ourselves. A broken heart is another. It seems sad and harsh, but it can't be helped. What, then, do we do with frailty and lack? How do we suffer honestly?

It can sometimes be extremely difficult to surrender to these situations, because we fear that if we do—if we even acknowledge what scares us—it is going to destroy us. So we are like the Little Engine That Could, puffing along with our positive thinking, always looking ahead, but afraid to look behind because something might be gaining on us. In fact, that something might not destroy but change us. The trouble is, the ego experiences change as death.

DJ: When I was in the hospital for Crohn's disease, there was a woman down the hall with the same disease who'd already had some thirty surgeries. The doctors wouldn't let her out of the hospital because she gave clear indications that she would commit suicide. I would never be so arrogant as to suggest that her mental attitude was wrong or that her disease was a metaphor. I think it's entirely possible that she just got the short end of the stick by developing an especially voracious disease.

MIB: You certainly can't be glib and say, "Oh, disease is just shadow material, so deal with it." God, no. It's overwhelming, awful. The stakes are very high.

In illness, you're suddenly not yourself anymore. The question is, are you going to cling in panic to some idealized self that no longer exists? Or are you going to cross the threshold and acknowledge that you're on a journey, though you don't know to where? You haven't chosen it, but now you're different in some way. This is one reason physical illness shows up as a turning point in so many spiritual biographies or as the catalyst of shamanic initiation. It's a profound shock to the system. It dislodges you. You look in the mirror, and one of the unfortunate ill stares back. But in a way, you could say that disease also abrades away, painfully, all of these superficial ways in which we judge our worthiness, even life's worthiness. Our worthiness, as in, "Am I strong, beautiful, competent, undamaged goods?" Or life's worthiness, as in: "Life is good only when it makes me happy, or aggrandizes me, or favors my enterprise." But who's bigger, you or life? There's a line in a Rilke poem Robert Bly translated: "This is how he grows—by being defeated, decisively, by ever greater beings."

This attitude contrasts with that of the new age movement, which supposes the mind can become sovereign over the body or "you make your own reality." The belief is that your pure intentions will make life happen in a particular way, enable you to control things. Now, intentions can be powerful, but I wonder if this overemphasis isn't fueled by a sense of outrage at the perceived injustice that we should be subject to the frailties of the flesh. If only we can make our spirits pure enough, our intellects bright enough, the new age seems to say, we shall never die. Death is perceived as an insult to our sense of ourselves as being a spirit or a mind.

We see the spread of this idea today in the immense popularity of people like Deepak Chopra, who has some valuable things to say, but is also a marvelous promulgator of the notion that if you just feel and think and live in a way that is absolutely congruent with God or spirit or whatever, then your obstacles, physiological or material, will vanish. And maybe they will, sometimes. But the greater challenge is to accept ourselves as we actually are and proceed from there.

DJ: I tried to read one of Chopra's books, but he seemed to regard death as the enemy.

MIB: I think any exploration of our relationship with disease—and, in fact, of our relationship with life—has to start with the understanding that we are going to die, that we are vulnerable, and that there are many other organisms striving for autonomy and health and self-fulfillment that are antithetical to us. We must start with the fact that no one is going to live forever, and that most of us fear this terribly.

Once we have accepted this as our starting point, we can then move toward another realization that goes hand in hand with the first: that death, as well as being our companion for life, is also a fundamental spiritual metaphor and a fundamental spiritual experience. Almost every tradition says you have to be "twice-born," and that death-and-rebirth pattern is not a single epiphanic event, but an ongoing process. To really live, you must die to your preconceptions. That's a spiritual axiom with a very long, august tradition behind it.

DJ: I recently had a dream in which anyone who had been severely burned was offered the opportunity to undergo an operation that would turn him or her into a seal. Some chose yes, some no. It's clear to me that this dream was about conscious choice. Once you've been severely ill, you can never go back to being how you were. You can either stay in this state of being sick, or you can "become a seal," which means to me that you can access depths previously denied to you.

MIB: Yes, exactly. The language of dreams is a "both/and" language, the antidote for our waking, logical "either/or." Taking dreams seriously means being able to exist in the depths and on the surface at the same time. In this realm, disease really does function as metaphor.

DJ: My book *A Language Older than Words* is about the language of the body. One of the means by which our bodies speak to us, I believe, is metaphor.

MIB: So often we view metaphors as secondary or derivative. But in Tibetan Buddhism, there is an arcane tradition called the Mahamudra, which sees everything as metaphorical, but not in the sense of things standing in for other things. Rather, it is said, "Things symbolize themselves." That is, the world is not your subjective fantasy, but it's not what we understand as "purely objective" either.

DJ: I see the world as a great dream, not unreal and immaterial, but alive and pregnant with meaning. To look at the world the way we look at our dreams, I think, would be to perceive it more as it really is.

MIB: Yes. If you see a horse in a field, you might not even pay attention to it; it's just another horse. But if you see a horse in a dream, you would likely ask yourself: What does that horse mean? Why is it here? The horse might have an incredible intensity or numinosity. It might even talk. Now, if we could bring that kind of perception to our waking existence, think of the richness of meaning that would greet us everywhere.

To get back to the relationship between the psyche and illness, what would happen if we perceived a symptom not just as an ache or pain to be avoided or alleviated, but as something that exists in meaningful relationship with us? I think that kind of a dialogue with symptoms is well worth the effort, and at the very least an attempt to engage with the world in a richer way.

In my case, I've had cancer in my thyroid. On the one hand, it's just a disease. On the other hand, it contains various levels of meaning. The latest research indicates that thyroid cancer is a civilizational disease. Atomic testing and excessive exposure to X-rays are among the only known causes. Kids growing up when I did, in the 1950s, drank radioactive-iodine-contaminated milk, and in a certain percentage of us, this has turned into so many internalized mini-Chernobyls. So there's social meaning.

Now, there are people who drank milk at the same table as I did who didn't get thyroid cancer. So although there's a direct cause—an etiology—there may also be other meaningful factors, such as the way I've lived my life, my habitual emotions and their repercussions in my body, and my attitudes and how they might have led to disease-promoting activities. And the organ itself and its location and function suggest issues surrounding voice, perhaps a sense of not feeling I could speak in my true voice. Or, since the thyroid produces the basic hormone that runs the entire metabolism, it may have had to do with how I use my energy. Certain patterns of living that came out of certain inner conflicts could have exacerbated my condition.

But we can also turn this idea on its head. Yes, I came to this disease with a preexisting set of psychological and spiritual habits. But instead of—or better, in addition to—asking whether any of these habits exacerbated the disease, I could have asked what I might have learned from this disease about these habits, and about my life, and even about life in general. I could have communicated with this new partner, this other to which I was now chained, like in an old movie where two escaped convicts are chained together: you may think you can knock the other guy into a river without getting dragged in yourself, but you can't. In the movies, the outcome is always that the convicts wind up talking to and learning from each other. Having exhausted all other options, they actually discover who the other is. Perhaps I needed to listen to my disease, and to the organ itself. Like most people, however, I found the whole situation confusing, and I kept trying to look at my condition as nothing other than an organic dysfunction.

DJ: A straight mechanistic approach.

MIB: Yes, even though a straight mechanistic approach conflicted directly with what, for example, my dreams were telling me.

DJ: When what you are told in dreams goes against what you are told elsewhere, how do you know what to believe?

MIB: It can be very difficult. The doctors said, for example, that the thyroid is a thermostat. (They often use mechanical metaphors.) But in my dreams, it was a starfish. I found that to affirm my own vision against the machine model created tremendous cognitive dissonance for me. Of course, there's no reason both metaphors can't work, but there was something deeper at stake.

In the dream, there was a sacred, intelligent starfish that represented—that was—my thyroid. That was the exact language of the dream: "sacred, intelligent starfish." And in the way that these healing dreams—sometimes called "big" or "numinous" dreams—seem to work, this one had a dimension of synchronicity with waking reality. The next day, on the spur of the moment, I went with my daughter to the Boston Science Museum, where I'd never been before. They happened to have an exhibit on starfish, and someone there put a starfish in my hand and said to me, "They can regenerate."

This spoke directly to the issue I was wrestling with at the time. Was it necessary to excise this organ? The conventional treatment was surgical removal, but I was asking if there was some way for it to heal. One message was coming from my dreams, the other from the world of medicine. I'm not sure, by the way, that even now I would blindly follow the advice of dreams, or recommend that anyone else do so, either; dreams can be very tricky. But here, at least, was this other country heard from, this countervailing attitude.

After that, I began to study my dreams intensively. I started keeping records, because these dreams were all so titanic and unprecedented in my own experience.

For probably five years, I spent an enormous amount of time going over them as if they were some kind of apocrypha I needed to understand. I found in my reading that many traditional cultures view the body's organs as living creatures having their own intelligences, their own voices. I started to see the body as a community of intelligent entities—which means, among other things, that I started to see it far less hierarchically. We normally see our conscious mind as the sole subject, and the body as an object. Therefore, we don't allow for any two-way communication.

But if we look more deeply into metaphor, we see that such two-way communication unquestionably happens through it. Metaphor is how the body and the psyche talk to the conscious mind. It's how the parts of the body—often through dreams—bring themselves into conscious awareness.

DJ: Where do dreams come from?

MIB: The medieval Hasidic commentator Amoli distinguished between the "Dreamweaver" and the "Master of Dreams." The Dreamweaver produces ordinary dreams, which are a rehash of waking life, what Freud called Tagereste, "the residues of the day." The Dreamweaver is probably close to our conscious mind, or just below it, in the subconscious.

But the Master of Dreams is another story. The more you look into what Jung called "big" or "numinous" dreams—dreams in which the dreamer is being spoken to—the more you find them infused with great wisdom. These dreams tend to be very vivid, with bright color and intense sounds. You get the sense you've been somewhere else. They're called "clear dreams" in some traditions, "true dreams" or "talking dreams" in others.

When I was trying to sort out my own big dreams, I would tell people, "It was a dream, but it wasn't a dream." I had no language to describe it. But then I studied Jung and looked at other cultures and discovered they all talk about it. Most commonly, they make a distinction between true dreams and ordinary dreams, or big dreams and little dreams. And the big dreams, the true dreams—whatever you want to call them—seem to come from a Master of Dreams, a source outside ourselves, which appears to be the basis for our idea of God.

DJ: So did the starfish dream come from the thyroid speaking to the dream master?

MIB: Well, we know the body and the brain talk to each other via neuropeptides and their receptors. But that is just a corner of a much larger picture. It seems to be a field effect—what Hinduism calls Indra's Web—where everything is somehow connected to everything else. We could say it's Rupert Sheldrake's "morphogenetic field," or Jung's collective unconscious.

DJ: The first interview I ever did was with Joseph Campbell. I asked him where archetypes come from, and he said, "Oh, obviously, the archetypes come from the organs." I was twenty-two at the time, and I thought he must have been losing his mind. It took me years to decide I agreed with him.

MIB: There's a great Jung quote to the effect that, although people think the archetypes are airy and spiritual, they're actually closely related to the instincts.

DJ: We still haven't answered the question of how dreams work.

MIB: I don't think we can.

DJ: I wonder if we could discuss the shadow a little more. It's so underrepresented in discussions of holistic health and spirituality.

MIB: OK, if you promise you won't think I'm being too negative. I'm usually unbearably cheerful, but we're in the realm of the unspoken here, a kind of forbidden zone.

Basically, we identify disease with outright evil and so believe it must be walled off, quarantined, carpet-bombed, not touched or thought about: "See no evil, hear no evil, speak no evil."

It's like after a nightmare: you wake up feeling horror and revulsion, not wanting even to acknowledge that you had this awful dream. You try to forget it, certainly not to look at it. These dreams become the things you cannot look at, like the gaze of Shiva, which burned off the head of Ganesh in Hindu lore. But then Shiva put an elephant's head on Ganesh, and he became one of the most beloved gods in the Hindu pantheon, a sort of wounded-healer figure.

Until some blast from Shiva comes along, we tend to operate according to the ego, which of course forms the surface of our entire social, cultural life. Suffering can crack that surface wide open, with unpredictable consequences. We're suddenly forced to live from the inside out.

Lately I've found myself drawn to the mystic Saint John. What I get from him is the idea that, until you are like Job on the dung heap, God will not speak to you. Some people see this idea as religious masochism, but I think what Saint John was getting at is the fact that only when you've suffered do you realize that your ego isn't running the show; and only then can this life force that is much larger than our conscious stratagems find a point of entry. It shows itself in those moments when we've been forced—or sometimes have chosen, through spiritual practice, to forsake the distorted pseudoself that usually gets us through life.

DJ: I agree with everything you're saying, except I would say it's not that God won't speak to us until we're naked on the dung heap; that's just the only time we will listen.

MIB: Yes, because God is always speaking. Illness or suffering can melt all that waxy buildup in our ears. Buddhists emphasize the active quality of ignorance: it's not that we don't know the truth. We do know it, but we actively push it away or ignore it. Both capital-T and small-t truth are coming at us constantly. It's just that we have effective antiballistic-missile systems to knock each particle of unwelcome truth out of the air before it even gets close to us. It's subliminal. This eternal vigilance costs us our freedom.

An Australian shaman once said to me that this voice—truth, knowledge, God, whatever you want to call it—is soft, like a butterfly on your finger; you could flick it off with an absent motion and lose it, just like that. We wish truth would grab us by the lapels, but we have to come to it. Sometimes this happens through voluntary attunement, a moral decision, but usually it's good old Shiva.

DJ: So disease, such as your thyroid cancer, can transform us personally. What about as a society?

MIB: The social aspect of disease is actually the one that interests me most. In traditional cultures, if one is sick, all are sick. But in the Western nations, we consistently ignore the collective nature—and collective cause—of disease. In fact, we don't recognize the cause at all. We live in this amazing consensual delusion, with people dropping like flies all around us—everybody knows somebody who is dying of cancer—yet we refuse to acknowledge that we are in the midst of a pandemic.

I spent a year trying to answer just one question: how do we identify causes and cures of cancer, or of anything else? For me, the cause of cancer ultimately comes down to industrial civilization and the machine that runs it. Cancer is a civilizational plague that arises directly from the way we live, the things we consume, the patterns that are imposed on us, or that we accede to, and that bear us along like a cultural conveyor belt. The machine that is late-industrial civilization is grinding people up limb by limb.

DJ: Or organ by organ.

MIB: And we keep seeing cancer as something that "just happened" to poor Aunt Gracie because of bad luck, or because she had that cancer gene. But we've had the same genes for maybe fifty thousand years, and there hasn't been a cancer crisis before the modern era. Sure, cancer's always been around: they've found it in Egyptian mummies and the roots of it in primitive organisms. And it's more prevalent now in part because we're living longer, and the likelihood of cancer increases with age. But there's never before been a pandemic like the one we see around us.

Albert Schweitzer was astonished when he went to Africa and found that the people there didn't have cancer. Today there would be genetic studies done on those tribes to determine what grants them this amazing immunity to cancer. But it's not a matter of immunity. These so-called cancer genes emerge under duress, with too many stressors to the organism and its immune system. That's a biological fact that gets left out of all the accounts of the salvation that genetic engineering will supposedly bring.

DJ: If cancer is a civilizational disease, then what's the cure?

MIB: Well, it's not just genetic fixes. If we want to sustain our collective life, spiritual and physical, on this planet, we need to transform our society, which employs people to produce toxicity in exchange for tawdry consumer baubles. It's as though we live in a world where the most profitable industries manufacture an invisible poison gas, and people are dying left and right, and whole medical specialties are devoted to finding antidotes to the poison gas, yet no one asks, "Why don't we stop manufacturing the gas?" Instead, someone is made a hero for inventing a better gas mask. The ultimate cure isn't technological inventions; it's stopping the problem at its source.

My town, Boulder, Colorado, is a nuclear-free zone. I've thought a lot about the idea of creating "cancer-free zones." Why couldn't we do whatever it takes to rid our towns of cancer? What would that take? What would it mean in terms of individual lives and the collective life of a community? To begin with, it would mean examining what it is we're doing and desiring that is fueling this threshing engine.

If the causes of the cancer pandemic are collective social factors, then the cure must be collective and social. In tribal cultures, they try to heal not just the sick person but the family, the society, the ancestors, the relationship to the gods— most of which are identified with the natural world. To even begin to think about this is a step toward building a stronger bridge between health practitioners and the environmental movement—one that goes beyond temporary alliances around "cancer clusters" near toxic-waste sites and the like.

Ultimately, the cancer crisis is a crisis of love: love in the deepest, nonnarcotic sense; love as ineluctable connectedness, as sensitivity to the nuances of the other and tenderness toward all living things.

DJ: Do you think we'll ever see a large-scale transformation of society?

MIB: The underlying paradigm is the hardest thing to change. You can nibble away at it here and there, but even your nibbling can be used to fuel the desire machine. Hence, the trend toward fast-food, one-stop-shopping spirituality, which is just one more frantic attempt to escape, one more instance of mistaking the finger pointing at the moon for the moon. This "spirituality" might open a door, but in the end it may do little more than provide analgesic comfort amid the existing pattern of narcissistic consumerism: "Be a happy, enlightened consumer."

As in individual healing journeys, I don't see us changing our way of being until the current pattern stops working—though many of us think it already has—and things become worse. You have to shudder to think what worse might look like. Many people, of course, have their eyes open to how dire the situation has become, and are starting to find effective ways of channeling that awareness.

In my own case, at least, I marvel at the possibility of looking at our existing condition as the raw material of enlightenment. It's like the old Buddhist saying, "In the poison is the medicine." There is tremendous magic just in relinquishing category. A lot of the talk is about building a better you, whether as individuals or as a society, but I think so often when we go that route—even with the best intentions—we end up erecting some new monuments that are going to topple over. We try to decorate them, shore them up, gild them, when what we really need to do is pull them down, or even just let them fall apart, and see what green and living shoots, what new organic models emerge.

DJ: One of my favorite phrases is, "Under the pavement, grass."

MIB: These forces of light and life are inexorable and ever present, but we struggle so hard to ignore them and maintain the status quo. Much of the civilization in which we live is the result of a refusal to see, or to listen: to the imagination, to our fellow beings, to the woundedness we all feel, which could change the world if we just acknowledged it. It's as if we've created this whole deafening way of living just to make sure we can't hear this thing that can be so quiet, as quiet as a butterfly. Our defense industries, goodies factories, light-speed lifestyle, and media oversaturation are all arrayed to cover up this gentle, quiet sound. But all the din and clatter of the world can never drown it out. It is always there, as close as our own breath.

JANE CAPUTI

Interview conducted at her office
at Florida Atlantic University,
Boca Raton, Florida,
October 30, 2001.

The work of Jane Caputi offers a cultural critique that starts with the deep interior of our intimate experiences and extends to the mythic landscape of the cosmos. From the personal to the political, we live in a rape culture, she argues, where pornography is the core story underlying militarism, planetary destruction, and racism, as well as violence against women. The body of the earth, once universally respected as the source of life, is daily violated and conquered along with anyone identified with nature, dirt, sex, or the wild. As Caputi makes clear, this conquering must be enacted in the mythic realm as well as the physical plane. And so, in popular culture serial sex killers are heroes, while goddesses—whether in the form of sharks, aliens, or femmes fatales—are slaughtered. This violence is "a ritual of enforcement, a form of terrorism." As Caputi writes, "All of this destroys any possibility of communication or entering into communion with anyone." It is also destroying the planet. Caputi's work is a clarion call to abandon domination as a cultural aspiration, and reclaim a biophilic mythos that can weave humans back into our place as exuberant animals in a creative, animate cosmos.

Jane Caputi is a professor of women, gender and sexuality studies at Florida Atlantic University. She has written three books, all against patriarchal domination: *The Age of Sex Crime; Gossips, Gorgons and Crones: The Fates of the Earth;* and *Goddesses and Monsters: Women, Myth, Power and Popular Culture.* She collaborated on *Websters' First New Intergalactic Wickedary of the English Language* with Mary Daly. She also has made a short documentary film, *The Pornography of Everyday Life,* and is now working on a new one, *Green Consciousness: Re-Attachment to the Mother/Earth.*

Derrick Jensen: You've written, "Rape is a social expression of sexual politics, an institutionalized and ritual enactment of male domination, a form of terror which functions to maintain the status quo."

Jane Caputi: I think the case has been made consistently by feminist theorists since the 1960s that rape is a political act, that common mythology aside, it's not a crime of desire, passion, frustrated aggression, victim provocation, or uncontrollable biological urges. Nor is it something done solely by deviants. Nor is it inexplicable within the culture. Instead it's a ritual of enforcement, a form of terrorism. Women live with the fear every day that if you're out at night you could be raped. If you're at home, you could be raped. If you're on the job and somebody doesn't like you, you could be sexually harassed or raped. These are realistic fears faced every day by women. They happen all the time.

DJ: The gold standard among studies, by Diana E.H. Russell, suggests that 25 percent of all women in this country are raped within their lifetimes, and another 19 percent have to fend off rape attempts.

JC: The assault is relentless. It's like Andrea Dworkin said: "Under patriarchy, gynocide is the ongoing reality of life lived by women." Kate Millett talks about how we so often think of patriarchy as a system of socialization so complete—it has so long and universally prevailed in the dominant culture and we so assent to its values—that you'd think it would no longer require violence to keep it in place. But the control of women by men would be impossible without this constant and everyday use of force. Rape is a way of forcing women to stay in their place.

Obviously, rape is not the only way women are forced to stay in their place. Forty percent of all women murdered in this country are killed by their sexual partners—husbands and boyfriends. And of course, women are killed at random, too.

I haven't actually written quite so much about rape as such, since that's been covered so well by so many others. Instead my first book examined modern serial sex murders, not only as a manifestation of gynocide, but as a mythic/ritualistic act in contemporary patriarchy.

DJ: You've written, "For the sexual killer—no matter how hypocritically reviled by his patriarchal culture—should be recognized finally as its 'ultimate man,' its subliminal hero, the inevitable enactment of phallocracy's most fundamental conceptions of manhood and godhood."

JC: This morning I was reading Sara Herdy's book on motherhood, in which she writes about the necessity within patriarchal cultures for female modesty and chastity as a means for men to own women and children. In order to keep this ownership in place, many cultures have had various kinds of enforcers. These enforcers have often been associated with the supernatural. Men dress up, paint themselves, take on these supernatural roles, then come and harass or kill women. The mythology of one culture states that the culture used to be a matriarchy, but the men decided the women had gone too far, and massacred all the powerful women. By saying the women had "gone too far," the men were blaming the women for their own victimization. This is something that is all too common within our own culture as well.

DJ: She was asking for it.

JC: And from that point on, if any woman got a little too uppity or out of her place, or a little less than modest and chaste, she would be attacked and killed by these spirits, whom the men impersonated.

So the notion of mythical figures terrorizing women is absolutely not unique to twentieth-century culture. We can also put the witch trials into this category of mythical enforcers terrorizing women for political and social purposes.

That said, there is still something new about the serial sex killer. He takes on a supernatural dimension. In fact, he becomes God. Here is an image of God the omnipotent, God the ultimate enforcer, the ultimate dominator, holding power of life and death in a way that is the very quintessence of a patriarchal vision of God. Not God as the sustainer, creator, transformer of the universe, but God as the one who could kill you, the one with the power of death over you. And not only death, but a very specific kind of death: death by domination.

One of the characteristics of patriarchy is the fusing of sex and violence. Sex, within a male supremacist culture, is, like everything else, constructed and defined in male supremacist terms. Thus, within a culture based on systematic subjugation of all that has been defined as feminine, it should come as no surprise that sex is systematically used to this purpose—to subjugate women—in private relations, through pornography, through sexual harassment, and so on. This patriarchally defined sex, although it's frequently mystified as love, eroticism, fantasy enactment, and the "natural" expression of dominance and submission, becomes synonymous with and indistinguishable from violence, pain, force, humiliation, and domination. In the same way, violence, pain, force—all of these are everywhere eroticized, suffused with sexual meaning and drama.

DJ: You've quoted Brian De Palma, director of such films as *Dressed to Kill, Carrie,* and *The Untouchables,* as saying, "I'm always attacked for having an erotic, sexist approach—chopping up women, putting women in peril. I'm making suspense movies! What else is going to happen to them?" Even more to the point, he also said that "using women in situations where they are killed or sexually attacked" is simply a "genre convention . . . like using violins when people look at each other."

JC: A 1984 study revealed that one in eight commercially-released films in this country depicts violent acts by men against women. As De Palma said, it's a genre convention. It's a convention, too, in advertising, where on the pages of *Vogue, Harper's Bazaar,* and so on we routinely see women dead, laid out, suffocated, shot, run over by cars, dismembered, all to advertise products like stockings, perfume, and shoes. Rock 'n' roll lyrics, music videos, billboards, display windows—all these contain routine violence against women. This violence against women truly is a "genre convention" in our culture. And of course the violence is oftentimes sexualized.

Serial sex killers, then, are the essence of patriarchy, the bringing together of sexualized violence in a way that goes even beyond rape. These killers often do not have sex with their victims, but rather substitute a weapon for their penis. And they often cut off or mutilate genitals or breasts.

DJ: Serial killers aren't the only ones to mutilate genitals or breasts. Until I read your work, I'd never made the connection between these mutilations and unnecessary hysterectomies and mastectomies.

JC: That's an important connection that has been made by others as well. It's a legal form of mutilation. I'm not saying that no woman has ever needed a hysterectomy, but we know that there are many unnecessary ones. Especially soon after the operations were developed they were often used to "treat" not only physical symptoms, but mental or emotional "disorders" as well. One list of symptoms to be so cured reads: "troublesomeness, eating like a ploughman, attempted suicide, erotic tendencies, persecution mania, simple 'cussedness' and dysmenorrhea." Troublingly, desire was considered a symptom requiring female castration. Other "mental disorders" requiring surgical cure included masturbation, contraception, abortion, and orgasm. In the 1980s, there were about 690,000 hysterectomies performed each year in the United States. Several medical studies done between the 1940s and 1970s reported that at least one-third of all hysterectomies had been performed on women with normal uteri. In many cases the women had presented no symptoms at all before surgery. We might keep in mind that as late as the 1980s 97 percent of all American gynecologists were men.

There are a couple of points to be made here. The first is that we might ask ourselves whether male surgeons would be so quick to cut were they instead mutilating or removing male organs. The second is that it is everywhere agreed, for example, that Jack the Ripper's desire to possess the uteri of women he killed was abhorrent. Yet what do we make of the actions of doctors who have often for no better reason also removed this same organ?

We can make similar arguments concerning unnecessary breast surgeries, by which I'm not just talking about breast enhancement. We also know that treating early breast cancer with radical mastectomies, which are mutilating and very damaging to the women who undergo them, doesn't just come from good medical practice, it also comes from animosity.

DJ: I understand what you're staying, but I don't yet understand the leap to the mythical.

JC: The leap to God comes when you get the extreme form of the patriarchal enforcer—the serial sex killer—suddenly taking on mythic and divine proportions. Jack the Ripper is the most obvious case, somebody now understood as having become in a sense immortal, understood as in essence worshipped, understood as inspiring followers, as having ultimate power over life and death, who plays the role of a hero, a mask that can be assumed by ordinary men in some kind of a fantasy. That's why we have all these continuing plays and stories and movies about Jack the Ripper, including the latest one, *From Hell*. Now, somebody might say to me, "The reason we have all these movies is that he's the epitome of evil." Well, he may be evil, yeah, but he's also certainly extremely attractive, he's certainly worshipped, there's certainly a whole lot more said about him than there is about any notion of the good.

DJ: Certainly more than about his victims.

JC: Accounts of him often go through what I would call the Hannibal Lecter treatment, where he starts out as the bad guy, but by the end he's become a romantic hero, and the woman he's terrorized is even supposed to marry him. What's happening here is that something is put up putatively as evil, as something negative, as something bad—just as rape is supposed to be a crime—but instead is glamorized, romanticized, heroized, and I would argue even deified, because it so strongly enforces the rules of power in the culture, enforces misogyny, enforces the defeat and subjugation of the feminine, which is encapsulated in women but exists in men as well.

DJ: Why must the feminine be defeated?

JC: When you create patriarchal masculinity as hard, cold, aggressive, dispassionate, objectifying, you're creating a rapist, you're creating a soldier, you're creating a terrorist. But men know this violence could be turned against them just as easily. Men get raped as children, in prisons, on the streets. It happens. But women everywhere must be said to be the sex that is open, penetrable, rapable. Not men.

Think about prison. Often when men are raped in prison, they are feminized. Everyone would say—and they would say—that they are deliberately being made into women. What is a woman? A woman is not so much someone born with biological XX chromosomes or a vagina, but somebody who is cast in the role of the one who is both penetrable and who is supposed to carry the burden or the waste of the one who is doing the dominating. It is only through her negation that he can be defined as positively masculine; how can he be a dominator if there is no one for him to dominate? And she can be played by a man or by a woman.

DJ: You quote Catherine MacKinnon: "Man fucks woman, subject verb object."

JC: That line stopped me in my tracks when I first saw it. It makes clear the deep gender roles that are assigned, the way all subjectivity is assumed by the masculine position, and that any time someone acts, even if the person is a woman, the one doing the acting is seen as the man, the masculine. The one acted upon, the receptor, is feminine.

DJ: It's also almost impossible to talk about male-female sexuality in a way that keeps the woman as subject in the sentence. The man says, "I want to be inside of you," or the woman says, "I want you to be inside of me." She's still the object. We don't really have the language for her to say, "I want to be around you," or for him to say, "I want for you to be around me."

JC: It's very phallocentric. The penis is the storyteller, the agent of all action. To break out of that is like trying to start a new language. You're going to be seen as deviant.

There's something else about "Man fucks woman, subject verb object." *Fuck* is the ultimate verb. It never fails to blow my mind that the same word that supposedly means I make love to you means I could do gross terrible violence to you. The whole paradigm of an exploitative, silencing, and objectifying relationship joining sexuality and violence comes together in that word. The whole of patriarchy is caught in four letters: it's the paradigmatic verb of this culture.

And even though men are of course very penetrable, even within consensual sexual relationships, it is terribly shameful for a man to be fucked, to be feminized, to be made into a woman.

The other day I was reading *Newsweek* and saw an ad for an SUV with copy reading, "Next time you go out to the wilderness alone, remember one word: *Deliverance.*" They're using the threat of male rape to sell SUVs to men, so when they go into the wilderness, they'll be impenetrable, encased in this hard object. It makes me wonder about this whole drive to build bigger and bigger SUVs, and bigger and bigger buildings, and to pave over the world. Is it really fear of rape? Because men know, once again, that they've created this abusive masculinity which they've turned against everyone else, and which could be turned against them.

Certainly something else they're afraid of—perhaps even more profoundly than getting a dose of their own violence—is the feminine within themselves, the chaos represented by the wilderness. When a man rapes a woman, while he is obviously raping a real woman, he is also attempting to rape away any element of the feminine in himself. And so men create this armor of masculinity, and then this armor of the SUV to inhabit, and they pave over the whole world not so much because they feel that they're so powerful, but because they feel themselves to be weak, and potentially dominated.

DJ: I think another reason we fear the wilderness and the feminine is that it reminds us of what we lose inside our shells. Richard Drinnon has this great bit in *Facing West: The Metaphysics of Indian-Hating and Empire-Building* about how one reason the Pilgrims had to kill the Pequots is because so many Pilgrims were running off dancing with Indians.

JC: Exactly. Because the good attracts. Similarly, we see lots of men who want to become women. There have always been feminine men, heterosexual and gay, drag queens. Men who want to cross-dress. There must be an incredible attraction for these men to do so, given the extraordinary oppression that they have to face because of it.

I need to be really clear that I'm not saying that women are good and men are bad. I'm saying that there is an attraction to the good, and that these good qualities have been labeled within patriarchy as feminine, but that they exist both in men and in women. And the reason that nature and creatures are seen as feminine, as all oppressed people are seen as feminine, is because the feminine is seen as a repository for everything which is disowned and projected outward by the oppressor.

DJ: Why?

JC: That's the question everybody always comes down to. What caused this in the first place? Is there some deep trauma in the psyche of domineering men?

DJ: My father was abusive, and it seems pretty clear that one reason he did violence to us was that he had to control his surroundings because he was so frightened. He, too, had been abused as a child.

JC: It's a truism that people don't bully and dominate because they feel themselves to be powerful. Their identity comes out of projecting everything they despise onto us and then trying to destroy it. And then their identity is completely linked to that role of dominator. This is one reason an abusive husband very often falls apart when his wife leaves him: he has no identity other than that. He's the weak one.

DJ: How does that make him weak?

JC: He needs her. Abusers dump all of their negative feelings of shame, of feeling dirty, of feeling weak, of feeling incapacitated, of having no self, onto those they abuse, who then carry the feelings for them.

DJ: I was talking to a psychologist friend who suggests that oftentimes abusers specifically seek out those who are most sensitive, and most willing to take on their shame.

JC: And better able to process it for them. Part of that willingness to take on that role of carrier or processor comes from having been acculturated into that role of being the recipient, a role once again associated with the feminine. Cleaning up after everyone. Processing everyone else's waste. People talk about the cliché of prostitutes with hearts of gold, but what is this alchemical thing they do? They take somebody's waste and turn it back into gold for them, so that the other leaves the encounter feeling renewed, while the prostitute is not only stigmatized as the filthiest member of society but carries so much of that affective burden that often her life is shortened by it. It's a hard life.

Environmentalism and feminism really meet around the notions of filth and dirt. Why should dirt be so degraded, why is being called dirty bad? When did dirt become a dirty word?

One reason oppressors feel themselves dirty—and so need to rid themselves of dirt—has to do with the standards of civilization. In order to be civilized, in order to be more like God, you have be transcendent, you have to be away from the earth, you have to be away from the dirt, you have to be away from the animal. This means that our animal parts, our sex organs, are the ones that are seen as the most dirty, the most shameful. And of course the moment of ejaculation is to the patriarch the most shameful of all, the most disgusting, because at that moment he is out of control; he is no longer a manly man. To be civilized is to be in control.

To be civilized is to hold oneself in opposition to nature, which is to hold oneself in opposition to oneself, to be ashamed of the animality of the self, which to the fully civilized means the "filth" of the self. All of this destroys any possibility of communication or entering into communion with anyone but other civilized humans. If we listen to the creatures and to the elements, and even to our bodies, we are then primitive, backwards. So we learn very early to put that away. We learn to despise ourselves and to feel ashamed of our bodies, to hate the dirt and to hate everything about us, because we're human, which means we're humus: the words come from the same Latin root meaning earth and dirt. But self-loathing is a difficult thing to acknowledge—maybe the most difficult—so all those characteristics we must loathe if we are to be civilized, if we are to dominate, get dumped into others who bear the shame and who end up feeling dirty.

The way to heal this is not to say to the dominator, "Keep your filth," but to say that we're all equally dirty, and dirt is great. To celebrate dirt. Think about how when we were kids we loved being dirty, how much we hated to be clean. It's a form of listening to the elements, coming into close contact with the earth. We have to start honoring that again. I believe it is that dissociation from the dirt that leads, ultimately, to sexual abuse. We have a hatred of the body, hatred of the self, shame about sexuality, that we then have to dump onto another. We can dump this hatred verbally, of course, but sexual contact—intimate physical contact—is far more effective.

Which takes us back, really, to the mutilation we talked about before. Why this emphasis on mutilating the cunt? I think it has to do with what the cunt represents. *Cunt*, by the way, is a really old word that has only become obscene in the last three hundred or so years. Some linguists tie it to the word *yoni*, the Sanskrit word for vulva, which comes from a word that means "to connect," in terms of yoking, bringing things together, unifying. The whole idea of the phallus, on the other hand—and of course I mean this not as the literal penis, but the way that the phallus is enshrined in skyscrapers, weapons, nuclear missiles, and so on in both Freudian and Lacanian psychology—is to disconnect us, to individuate us by disconnecting us from the mother so we can gain individual consciousness. It seems to me that this sort of worship of the phallus and most especially what it has come to represent is a source of great cultural tragedy.

What we really need, and this is the theme of my new book, is cunctipotence, which means all-powerful. I'm reclaiming that word to mean female potency and possibility. Of course men can be cunctipotent, too: it means you have that state of consciousness that seeks connection, that understands that we really are all connected.

Years ago I was in Northern California and I saw a huge bird on a fence. I heard the bird say, "We all used to speak the same language, but you've forgotten that we really are all one being. That's why you can't understand our language anymore."

It's really an amazing thing to hear an animal speak. It comes in your mind as the whole message at once. Or at least that's how it comes to me. And it hasn't happened to me nearly often enough. I wish it would happen more.

We all have the ability to do that. We are not islands. We are extremely permeable. Cunctipoitence is about remembering that connectedness, that permeability, while maintaining our individual distinctiveness.

All of these things, like permeability, that are considered feminine and are despised, really are the nature of being. Something scared somebody somewhere somehow, and that person walled off, individuated, and said, "I'm not penetrable, you are."

DJ: If you hate a quality that is the nature of being, then you are hating the nature of being.

JC: And you have to destroy being. Which is one reason Jack the Ripper attacked the vulva, the source of life.

But it's more complex than this. The vulva also symbolizes—all over the world—the source of death. It is the womb and the tomb. Archetypally, it is the gate between the worlds. We come into being there, and it is also the mouth of hell, or the jaws of death. That's all vulva symbolism. It seems to me that when you attack the vulva you are not just attacking life and women, but also death. You are refusing the whole cyclic nature of being, the transformative nature of being, as if you could just step back from that and individuate, control, separate, and fix nature and being.

DJ: Thomas Berry once said to me that while everything is sacred, transitions are especially sacred. The transition between day and night, the transition between waking and sleeping.

JC: Zora Neale Hurston said the horizon is the biggest thing god ever made. I think they're saying the same thing.

DJ: So, since birth and death are the biggest transitions in a life, to desacralize the vulva is to desacralize transitions.

JC: That brings us to pornography, because that's what pornography is all about: desacralization, profaning the sacred.

It's really difficult. Fundamentalist religions push female modesty, saying, "Oh, the body is sacred. That's why it has to be hidden and taboo and veiled." But that's not at all what I mean by sacred. First, both the penis and the vulva are sacred. And they're not even really that different. A small penis isn't that different from a large clitoris, and we all know how we're homologs of each other; different hormones enter at a certain stage in fetal development and you go one way or the other. We have much more in common than we do separating us. We're not opposite sexes at all. To believe we are opposite—in hierarchical opposition, as competitive and as existing in other worlds—is a great part of the problem. It seems much more useful—and accurate—to think about male and female, and other so-called opposites, like human and nonhuman, life and death, as complements.

Indians sometimes talk about how you can't really enter into a relationship with the natural world or have deeper experiences of communion just by going for occasional hikes, that the best you can hope for is a sort of aesthetic experience. I think we can describe pornography the same way. It's a visual screen. It also reverses an incredibly sacred moment in much of ancient iconography and myth, which is the baring of the vulva. Think of Isis sitting on top of a pig spreading her legs. Or we can return to Zora Neale Hurston. When she went to Haiti and was being initiated into voodoo, her guide/teacher asked her, "What is the truth?" She couldn't answer. He then answers his own question by telling the story of a ritual in which the elaborately-dressed mambo slowly strips, and ultimately reveals her vulva, saying, "This is the ultimate mystery, this is the source of all truth."

Now, I'm not saying that we should all get down and worship the vulva, but rather that we should understand that marked on our bodies, on our genitals, male and female, are those symbols of birth and death. These are also those places where the sacred power of the cosmos comes in really big. Why else do you think sex feels so good? All of that pleasure and power and energy is not just for creating new beings, but it is about exuberance and ecstasy and ebullience. That's the sacred power of the universe; that's what desire is. Desire in our bodies is our best talisman connecting us to whatever those generative forces are in the cosmos that keep the green coming in the spring and the stars turning and the earth wheeling around. That's why desire and the genitals are so powerful.

There's a great book called *Biological Exuberance: Animal Homosexuality and Natural Diversity*, by Bruce Bagemihl. In it, he writes about the fact that many animals have homosexuality, and that many indigenous peoples recognize gay people as sacred because there is this whole other force of exuberance in sexuality, this recognition and actualization of nonprocreative sexuality as a part of the nature of the cosmos, a sort of excess exuberance.

Alice Walker successfully gets at that in *The Color Purple*, when she displaces the old white man father God and tells Celie that praying is like having an orgasm. I really think she's right. I think sex is a form of prayer. Orgasm is a form of prayer. I grew up Catholic, and our prayers were, "Oh dear God, please take care of me." It was all about petitioning our Lord and Master for favors. But that's not it at all. Prayer is exchanging energy. And through lovemaking you are exchanging energy.

This ties also, as everything does, to the land. Through lovemaking you exchange energy not only with your partner, but with the land where you are making love. The land wants that. It wants you to participate in that flow, in that cunctipotence, that connection.

We have to feed the green. Normally we think of the green as just feeding us, the land as feeding us. But that's the same old petitioning God for favors, an infantile notion that we're just here to suck on the breast, to be fed, without giving anything back. We have to give back to the source. It's not that the green is dependent on us like we're dependent on them: it's proportional. But it is mutual.

The other day I was reading a guide for ecotourism in the *New York Times*. The suggestions were pretty basic: always clean up, always support the locals, don't ask a lot of stupid questions, express your gratitude. It set me thinking that these are good rules for all-around behavior, and I began fantasizing some kind of *Book of the Green*, where we begin to articulate a growing, changing, body of principles we can gather around as we restructure the destructive social system that surrounds us.

DJ: I'd like to return again to pornography. What's wrong with it, and what's the difference between pornography and erotica?

JC: Again, I'm indebted to a lot of other feminist thinkers on this subject, like Andrea Dworkin and Catherine MacKinnon. We've been talking here about hierarchical opposition, disconnection, and domination. Pornography is sexually-explicit material that eroticizes inequality, hierarchy, subordination. It doesn't necessarily have to have the sort of crudeness that we often associate with porn. I do a lot of work with what I call everyday pornography, images in mainstream media that use, for example, mutilated body parts to sell us eyeshadow or pantyhose or cars. We've been acculturated to see these images as normal, but they're really hideous. And pornography acclimates us to this stuff in the mainstream.

DJ: I'm thinking also of those rape scenes we see in movies all the time that begin with the woman pushing the man away and end with her arms around his back, like in *Dr. Zhivago*.

JC: The message is that women really want to be taken, women really want to be dominated. That's the work of pornography, whether or not it's sexually explicit: to eroticize oppression. Thus slavery, or torture, or the subjugation of women, of the feminine, can gain some kind of erotic charge. Pornography disconnects, it objectifies, so that you're not relating to another being, you're not participating in that energetic exchange we were talking about, you're not connecting, you're objectifying and thereby controlling, and not having to open up to any of those things in yourself. Also, it's addictive. It becomes a substitute for actual exchange.

DJ: I'm still not clear. What's wrong with a shot—a photograph—of a woman lying on her back with her legs spread, and how would that look different were it erotica?

JC: I think we need sexual depictions, because desire exists, and we like to have stories and pictures of food, or other important parts of our lives. But looking at pictures of food doesn't cause you to lose your taste for actual food. Pornography can cause you to lose your taste for actual relationship.

The important point is that a photograph of a woman on her back with her legs spread teaches us, first of all, because there aren't similar pictures of men around, that women are the class who are particularly sexualized in this way as accessible, as objects, as objects of desire, so that the bodies of women become subject to this kind of obsessive fixation as well as obsessive modesty. You wouldn't have this whole idea that women have to be completely covered unless it was thought that women were sex somehow, whose bodies evoke this kind of desire. Are men perceived the same way? No, of course not. If a man takes off his shirt, it doesn't cause a big stir. Why is that? It's because women's bodies have been charged with sex. Women's bodies are sex. Sex, the dirtiness of sex, the shame of sex, the out-of-controlness of sex, have all been projected onto the bodies of women. Where is the real woman in this picture? She disappears. The woman on her back with her legs spread has been rendered into a commodity that can be purchased. The picture teaches you that you can have a kind of sexual experience without having to give any of your own energy back to another being. It teaches you that you need not give her respect, nor that you even need acknowledge her existence. The photograph renders her as completely accessible, completely penetrable. Consumable. There is a whole tradition within our culture of women as objects to be consumed. Women as candy. Women as sustenance. And pornography reflects the way that this whole class of beings—women—are treated.

It's really strange and revealing that this can arouse us. I remember seeing pornography when I was a kid, and remember finding it arousing, in great measure I think because of my repressive Catholic upbringing, which prepared me for pornography, since I'd been forbidden any knowledge or experience of sex. And I think pornography is most powerful in an atmosphere of sexual repression. You're completely ignorant, you're starved for any kind of experience or knowledge, and then pornography comes in. But while it may arouse you, it doesn't prepare you for actual sexual engagement. It addicts you to that specifically-engineered thrill, and hampers your ability to deal with real people and real sexuality in real situations.

I don't think it's just porn that we get addicted to. We live in a way that leads to addictions. I was recently reading about a guy in *Newsweek* who said that in the wake of the September 11 attacks he was starting to watch news as if it were porn. He can't get enough of it. He tries to mute it when his children come into the room. He knows he's got some kind of unhealthy addiction going on right now to sensationalized stimuli that are playing on one of his survival drives, in this case fear. But he has been diverted by this addiction from actual day-to-day physical survival, and day-to-day communication with the flesh-and-blood people with whom he lives. He knows he's not really learning anything, but can't stop himself.

DJ: I would say that this sort of addiction to news-porn is more likely to spring up, too, when we are starving for real information, and starving, too, for real emotions in our own lives.

JC: And it's not just news. Porn is emblematic of our relationship to everything, and to the commodification of everything. We live in a world of surfaces, and we are directed to live in a world of surfaces. This is true whether we're talking about glossy pictures of women or sound-bite journalism or weekend outings in "the wilderness."

But there's something else I want to say about pornography, which is that it thrives on the idea of sex being dirty. This means I can never criticize porn without criticizing traditional morality. Traditional morality tells us that goodness is clean, ignorant, and asexual, like Forrest Gump. In the worldview that holds sexual and other forms of innocence as good, evil comes out through characters like Jack the Ripper, and is very sexualized. When the good is defined as asexual, where is the room for the sexual?

Pornography thrives also—because we have this taboo that sex is dirty and disgusting, and believe the body to be unintelligent—on the mind/body split. The mind—man—is intelligent, while the body—woman—is stupid and sexual. But the body is extremely intelligent, as is sexuality. And the mind is very sexual. All of these perceptions and ways of being in the world are lost—must be lost—when we live on the surface.

Pornography also turns upside down our relationship to the sacred and to nature. Think of "bitches," "pussies," all those words taken from the animal world. There are classic pornographic scenes of women having sex with animals. That is a perversion of something that used to be sacred: the connection of sexuality and women to animals. The goddess as the lady of the beasts has been profaned. The exposed vulva has been commodified. The dirt has been made shameful. All that was sacred in the ancient world has been turned upside down and made into symbols of degradation. And that causes us to lose the understanding that all aspects of our bodies are sacred, and all aspects of life are sacred.

DJ: I did some research into porn sites for a book. The part of each site I found the most interesting was the counter that records how many people have visited the site. Some of these places have had tens of millions of visitors.

JC: That shows the depth of starvation in the culture. They rob you of your connection to the elemental, and then sell it back to you as consumer objects and consumer porn.

DJ: When I was doing the research, I found that the images affected my spontaneous fantasy life in a way I didn't like. In the couple of months I was looking at them, I started doing something I'd never done before, which was to mentally undress women I saw. I'm really glad that stopped soon after I stopped visiting the sites.

JC: Why do you think it stopped?

DJ: In part because I was able to metabolize it through writing about it.

JC: What do you mean by metabolizing?

DJ: I took it into my body.

JC: Took what into your body?

DJ: I took the porn into my body, as I do everything I research, and then I converted it, the same way I convert food into energy, into the understanding I attempt to convey to readers, and then I shit out the rest of it.

JC: The reason I'm asking is because I've been thinking a lot lately about metabolism. So many people I respect talk about knowing or feeling things in their cells. Metabolism is the process of cellular transformation: taking in materials, converting them to energy, putting out waste. Metabolism has a really interesting etymology. *Boli* means devil, as in diabolical, coming from a root that means to throw, because the devil was something thrown across your path that would make you change direction, literally a demonization of change.

DJ: Which is a demonization of lack of control.

JC: Yes. It's all about chance, and attempting to eliminate chance. The first things all fundamentalisms outlaw are sexuality, music, and gambling or games of chance. Significantly enough, all of these are absolutely fundamental principles in the cosmos. The ancient world knew all of these as necessities, and within our culture we try to eliminate, regulate, or demonize them.

DJ: I want to go back to erotica, because we haven't really . . .

JC: . . . defined how erotica would be different.

There would have to be a sense of time and relationship in it, and connectedness. It wouldn't simply be a case of putting in a few props—her favorite books, for example—or anything like that. The problem goes beyond the photograph to the mindset that creates it, that leads to it, so if you have a pornographic mindset taking the picture, you're going to have a pornographic picture no matter what you do. The photograph would have to be taken by someone who was in a sense in a relationship with the subject (not object), and felt love and respect for the model, in which case it wouldn't really matter what props were or weren't used. The same is true for photographs of nonhumans. We know that pictures of animals can objectify them, and that pictures of the landscape can present it as something to be appropriated or invaded. Eroticism would respect the integrity of the being.

DJ: Given the depth to which we are all inculcated into the patriarchal mindset, I'd think that to see eroticism would be as confusing to us as it is to attempt to describe sexual relations where the woman is not the object of the sentence.

JC: Confusion is such an interesting state of being. It really just means to fuse with. And of course it's almost always assigned to the feminine; the feminine is confused, the masculine is completely ordered and straight. I actually really like confusion. It's demonized, and made to seem the worst possible state to be in, but isn't it true that chaotic confusion is the state out of which all creativity emerges? And isn't confusion the essence of the erotic? Is it you, is it me, who am I, who are you? That kind of merging is extremely powerful.

That's another problem with pornography. There's none of that confusion, that mingling of boundaries. We know which of us is gazing, and which of us is being gazed at. You're an object, I control you, I gaze at you, you operate according to my script.

This is all very dangerous, I might add, because pornography ends up merging our desire to the very system that oppresses us. How, then, could we ever rebel against it? If the only way we can get off is in dominant and subordinate situations, even if they're subtle, how will we ever really overcome this order? We would be giving up our sexuality. Feminists have always found that both women and men accuse us of taking their sexuality away from them, having no humor, having no pleasure, because all those things are so identified with domination and subordination, even if you're playing with those roles. So we get accused of being the ultimate killjoys, or prudes. But the truth is that all of that stuff is really already taking away your sexuality and putting it in the service of commodities. Look at how cars are sold as a sexual experience, so you don't have your own sex anymore; your sexuality is channeled into being gratified by owning that SUV. We're being ripped off. Deeply. And we can't fight the system because it's being fused back to us.

That's the thing about all of these oppressive systems: they have no energy of their own. They are completely contingent upon us for their energy. That's true even of a rapist. Nancy Venable wrote about this in her book *After Silence*. She was attacked by a stranger in the middle of the afternoon in her own home. He was terrorizing her, and taking in her terror as fuel, fueling his actual rape of her. She said that at a certain point she felt the detachment of a yogi come over her, and he began to lose energy and to lose the will and ability to carry out the rape any further. Then he started to become afraid. He started to feel his own fear, instead of being able to transmit it to her and then to feed back off of her fear. Now, I'm not saying that women who understandably feel fear when they are raped are doing anything wrong, nor am I saying that if the man starts feeling his own fear he might not respond with even more violence. I'm merely saying that all of these oppressive systems have no energy of their own. They're contingent upon being parasites on the oppressed. It's the colonial model.

DJ: I'm so glad that you said that, because I've always known that the dominant culture is a culture of parody, where pornography is a parody of sex, where heaven is a parody of present ecstasy, and so on all down the line.

JC: And if we could only realize that how different everything might be.

There's this amazing moment in the first *Nightmare on Elm Street*. The movie is really an initiation ritual, and a very powerful feminist statement, except that they tacked on an ending where Freddy Krueger, the monster, still lives. But the climax of the movie is where Nancy, the heroine, realizes that Freddy has no energy without her. She says, "I turn my back on you. I deny you." And she walks away. He completely collapses. He can't survive except with her energy. If we only could realize that. We take away our energy, and the system will collapse. It's already collapsing.

The other day I was down at the beach with a friend, and we looked around and didn't see a single bird. This was in Florida. Even a hundred years ago there were so many birds here that the sky would be darkened for days at a time. All over Florida. Often. In that moment I was gripped by the idea that the apocalypse has already happened. It probably happened thousands of years ago.

DJ: Hundreds.

JC: No, longer. I mean the original impulse that started the apocalypse. That's when it happened. It's not something in the future.

DJ: It's ongoing.

JC: No, it already happened. And we're living out the residue of that original apocalypse, which was probably first caused by that separation from the source, that denial of shared being. It's also clear to me that those creation myths that we say are all in the past are really in the future. They're telling us it's still possible to get the wisdom from the serpent. It's still possible to bite into the apple. It's still possible to dive down—as the frog did in a Hopi creation myth—and get that little bit of dirt and bring it up and put it on the back of the turtle so that the land will grow. That's what those myths are about. It's a reversal.

People sometimes ask me where I get my hope from, and I say that it comes from the understanding that the apocalypse isn't in the future, like the Bible says, nor is creation in the past. Instead, it is our task to begin living out those creation myths.

DJ: You've written a book called *Gossips, Gorgons & Crones: The Fates of the Earth*. How do these mythic figures play into this?

JC: We've been talking about relationships, which by definition involve listening. Listening is gossiping, in its old meaning, its true meaning. It comes from the words *god* and *sib*, as in sibling. Your gossip was your divine sibling, the person with whom you had a divine relationship, so that you could communicate on all levels. And of course it wasn't restricted to human beings. Just like an animal could be your familiar, your family member, with whom you have that bond, you could have an animal as your gossip, if you could find a creature who would take you on in that way. Here's an example of how gossip was used, from the *Oxford English Dictionary*: "She gossiped wisdom from the stars." Gossiping is really about learning how to listen to that language that connects us all, that makes us all siblings, all family. And the gossips, in mythology, are also midwifes, appearing at moments of new birth. This has everything to do with what we were just talking about: this restructuring that is going on following the collapse. It's like at the beginning of *Sleeping Beauty* where the wise women, the gossips, came to name gifts over the baby—you're going to be this, and you're going to be this, and you're going to be this. That's exactly what we need to be doing right now. Shaping the emerging world.

Something else we must do, and this is well inside the role of traditional gossips, is that we must speak about the unspeakable, specify and expose perpetrators, tell truths, satirize and ridicule, talk back, prophesy, foretell. And we must prepare ourselves to unthink the thinkable; that is, we must unthink nuclear war, environmental devastation, and so on. As gossips, we must gather, talk back, and refuse and refute these thoughts.

Of course, as with all forms of feminine power, gossiping has been devalued within our patriarchal culture, in this case reduced to bored busybodies (inevitably women) saying mean things to each other about people who aren't there to defend themselves. But that's a parody of its real meaning.

Now the Gorgon. We all know Medusa, right? The goddess with the hair of snakes. Supposedly very ugly. Face that could stop a clock, as they say. But she's ugly because all of the wisdom that she represents has been disowned. The snake, in the ancient world, is from the underworld. It sheds its skin and through that teaches us of life and death transformations. It speaks to us and offers us wisdom. All of which is why the Bible had to demonize it. There's an image of the Garden of Eden from the thirteenth century that shows the serpent in the Garden as Lilith, with female breasts, a crown, and the lower half of her body as the serpent. The serpent represents everything that we've been talking about—the dirt, the underworld, the sexual—that's been despised and disowned by patriarchal civilization. But the truth is that Medusa was a woman adorned with wisdom. And she and Athena were really the same goddess, but divided by the mind/body split we've been talking about. Athena became the virgin warrior—the chaste one, the fighter—and Medusa was the ugly, despised one. But they're both the goddess of wisdom.

Another part of the Medusa myth is that if you look at her she will turn you to stone. Her face is the marker of taboo. If you get too close, you are petrified. She is a reminder that ultimately we don't control the planet, and we can't do everything we may want. Okay, we can build these nuclear bombs, but nuclear waste is ultimately going to do us all in. The ozone hole. Global warming. The earth has its taboos, its own boundary-markers. The Gorgon reminds us that we have to ask permission. And if we are refused, we don't go in.

At the same time, the universe invites us into knowledge. That's what the Garden of Eden myth is about. The serpent handing Eve the fruit is a beautiful moment where the elemental world is inviting us to partake of its wisdom, which it gives us willingly, joyously, if we don't go in slashing and burning, trying to find the apple. That moment, too, has been demonized.

DJ: Let's talk about the Crone.

JC: The Crone, of course, is the old woman. In so many traditions—the Native Americans come to mind most readily—you have the understanding that all life comes to us from the grandmothers. We often have this image of the grandmother as this sweet old lady, and to be sure the Crone is nurturing and loving and all that, but she also is the figure who lays down the law. She is the ultimate boundary between the worlds. She is the face of death and transformation. Ultimately she is the face of change. Everything must change.

This is yet another piece of the earth and of ourselves which has been demonized. We, particularly women, are told we must stay young and fixed in this permanently sexually-desirable, fertile mode. That is in part because within our patriarchal system we have become afraid of the Crone. In many ways, the Crone has become the most denied and despised image, and the most hidden, because she ultimately signifies transmutation, which is so scary to so many of us. We're so very afraid of change.

But if we're all stuck denying the Crone, and denying dirt, denying darkness, denying death, what we get is this sterile Stepford world. Do you remember the movie *The Stepford Wives*? All the husbands killed their wives and replaced them with robots who were excellent housekeepers, great cooks, and always willing to be sexual partners. And they never aged. It's a classic patriarchal dream, that, as is true for so many patriarchal dreams, is actually a nightmare. I'll talk about that in a second.

But first I'd like to tell an Irish myth. In one of the myths of the sovereignty goddess, four brothers are hunting in the woods in Ireland. They're really thirsty, and they come to a well, next to which stands an old crone who is extremely ugly. The brothers ask, "Could we have a drink?"

She says, "You can have a drink, but you have to kiss me first."

Three of the brothers make disgusted faces, and say, "No, we don't want to kiss you." They leave. But the youngest brother says, "Sure, I'll give you a kiss." He kisses her, and they begin to make love. He's obviously fine, and happy to be with her. At that point, in the middle of their lovemaking, she changes into a beautiful young woman. He is completely shocked, and asks, "What's your name?"

She says, "My name is Sovereignty." This is because everything is all according to her will. They may drink or not, at her will. She will make love with them or not, at her will. She will be young or old, at her will. And she names him king. The point is that she is the spirit of the land who guards the sacred well, which is the source of all life.

But there's another point here, too, which is that her cycling of old and young is crucial to the life force. You have to go through birth, life, death, sustenance, decay, rebirth.

What we ultimately get from our denial of the Crone, from our whole pornographic fixation—that we're always young, that we're always fertile—are ultimately these images we have of women in the future, of Fembots in high heels. Did you ever notice how they're so often dressed in white? That's because they're sterile. The Stepford Wife really is the ultimate death face, because she's completely sterile. The men who killed their wives—who killed off the living women—thought they'd won, because they could fuck their cleaning and cooking and fucking machines any time they wanted. But the Stepford Wives did not have the capacity to cause life to continue. And of course I am not only talking about women, but how we perceive all of nature, and what we are trying to create.

Ultimately the goddess, and I don't mean some woman up there in the sky, but the force of life, is always in charge. So this means if we disrespect the lifeforce long enough, we end up bedded down with a pornographic doll, a Stepford Wife, nothing that can bear new life into being. That is the ultimate apocalyptic image.

DJ: You're clearly interested in language. Could you respond to a line you quote by Julia Penelope? "Language is an intangible, almost invisible weapon. Its messages are implanted in our minds when we are babies, and left there to maintain our allegiance to men and their institutions."

JC: Language is double-edged. It can be that kind of weapon—for example the "man fucks woman" stuff we talked about—but more and more, particularly after working with Mary Daly, it's becoming increasingly clear that even though the English language has done its best to kill the spirit of words—who are entities, angels, ensouled beings—the words haven't died.

DJ: I don't understand.

JC: We don't merely say words. They speak to us. And we learn from them. They carry history.

I don't think of words so much as weapons anymore. I know they can work that way when they are possessed, when they are made into pornographic replicas of themselves—for example, naming a whole group of people as evildoers. But I have found my richest musings come by looking into the backgrounds of words, tracing them back through the dictionary, seeing connections among them.

For example, the subtitle of the book we were just talking about is *The Fates of the Earth*. I had a hard time coming up with a subtitle, and one day I was out in the woods and thought of Jonathan Schell's book, *The Fate of the Earth.* His title had always seemed kind of wrong to me, because it implied that elite or military men held the fate of the earth in their hands. But the belief that we hold the fate of the whole earth in our hands comes out of the same kind of arrogance that created nuclear weapons with no forethought about what we're going to do about the waste. We're not that powerful.

The earth has Fates all her own. The earth has purpose. And we can only partially know what that purpose is. So I wanted to reverse our understanding of it, our usage of that word, just like we need to reverse the notion of who is doing environmental work, or any of the other work on this planet. We think we're doing it all. But the animals are doing the real work of holding it all together, and keeping us on our path. As are the plants. It's as if we think the stars and sun and moon and the earth itself aren't doing any work. It's as if we think that all of nature is unintelligent except for us. Well, the earth has intelligence and purpose and fates all her own. And those are really the primary fates.

DJ: I like what you're saying, but I can see that being misused very easily by someone saying, "Well, if the earth has fates of her own, and if the fate of the earth really isn't in the balance . . ."

JC: Why do anything?

DJ: Exactly.

JC: Oh, but this calls upon us to have tremendous responsibility: it is our responsibility to participate in those Fates. We're part of the earth. It is up to us to be in alignment with those purposes, not to go against them, nor to sit back and pretend. You have to give back. You have to participate in those Fates, because they are your Fates as well.

DJ: How do we know what to do?

JC: The Fates pull us. They have an attractive power, like gravity. It's that attraction to the good. Because giving in to that attraction involves letting go of our control, and letting go of our illusions of control, it is, within a patriarchy, the scariest thing we could be asked to do. So often in popular mythology giving in to these Fates is presented as wrong or evil. Think about the Borg queen in *Star Trek: First Contact*. They're all attracted to her. She's the femme fatale. Everyone is dying to be with her. But she's evil, and so you have to kill her, get rid of her. No! The Fates are good. And they attract us because that attraction is attracting us to our purpose, and toward the good.

If we could only just remember the ancient philosophical principle, that the good attracts, we could realize that these creation myths are attracting us for the future, calling upon us to take up our responsibilities, to bring that creation into being. Because creation is ongoing and collective, and we participate in it.

PAUL STAMETS

Interview conducted
by telephone, June 27, 2007.

For several years people from different places and backgrounds kept recommending the same oddly titled book to me: Paul Stamets's *Mycelium Running: How Mushrooms Can Help Save the World* (Ten Speed Press). Everyone told me it was one of the most mind-bending texts they'd ever read. With so many recommendations, I perversely hesitated to pick the book up, and when I finally did, I prepared myself to be disappointed.

I wasn't. Stamets fundamentally changed my view of nature, and in particular, fungi: yeasts, mushrooms, molds, the whole lot of them.

When we think of fungi, most of us picture mushrooms, those slightly mysterious, potentially poisonous denizens of dark, damp places. But a mushroom is just the fruit of the mycelium, which is an underground network of rootlike fibers that can stretch for miles. Stamets calls mycelia the "grand disassemblers of nature" because they break down complex substances into simpler components. For example, some fungi can take apart the hydrogen-carbon bonds that hold petroleum products together. Others have shown the potential to clean up nerve-gas agents, dioxins, and plastics. They may even be skilled enough to undo the ecological damage pollution has wrought.

Since reading *Mycelium Running*, I've begun to consider the possibility that mycelia know something we don't. Stamets believes they have not just the ability to protect the environment but the intelligence to do so on purpose. His theory stems in part from the fact that mycelia transmit information across their huge networks using the same neurotransmitters that our brains do: the chemicals that allow us to think. In fact, recent discoveries suggest that humans are more closely related to fungi than we are to plants.

Almost since life began on earth, mycelia have performed important ecological roles: nourishing ecosystems, repairing them, and sometimes even helping create them. The fungi's exquisitely fine filaments absorb nutrients from the soil and then trade them with the roots of plants for some of the energy that the plants produce through photosynthesis. No plant community could exist without mycelia. I've long been a resident and defender of forests, but Stamets helped me understand that I've been misperceiving my home. I thought a forest was made up entirely of trees, but now I know that the foundation lies below ground, in the fungi.

Stamets became interested in biology in kindergarten, when he planted a sunflower seed in a paper cup and watched it sprout and lift itself toward the light. Somewhere along the way, he developed a fascination with life forms that grow not toward the sun but away from it. In the late 1970s he got a Drug Enforcement Administration permit to research hallucinogenic psilocybin mushrooms at Evergreen State College in Washington. Stamets has studied mycelia for more than thirty years, naming five new species and authoring or coauthoring six books, including *Growing Gourmet and Medicinal Mushrooms* (Ten Speed Press) and *The Mushroom Cultivator* (Agarikon Press). He's the founder and director of Fungi Perfecti (www.fungi.com), a company based outside Olympia, Washington, that provides mushroom research, information, classes, and spawn—the mushroom farmer's equivalent of seed. Much of the company's profits go to help protect endangered strains of fungi in the old-growth forests of the Pacific Northwest.

Derrick Jensen: Your most recent book is called *Mycelium Running: How Mushrooms Can Help Save the World*. Can we start by talking about what is mycelium, and then talk about how they can save the world?

Paul Stamets: Well, a mushroom is the fruitbody of the mycelium, which is the network of thin cobweb-like cells that infuses all soils. The mushroom is called the fruitbody because it's the reproductive structure visible to the naked eye. In the mushroom are spores, somewhat analogous to seeds. And this fleshy and oftentimes succulent structure is attractive to animals, including insects. It's nature's way of offering a fungal bouquet of food to attract animals and other organisms who help spread the spores. Flies, squirrels, humans, bears are all attracted to fungi—and specifically to mushroom-forming fungi—because they're so rich in nutrients as well as fragrances, and these creatures all participate in the spreading of fungal spores.

There are an estimated one to two million species of fungi, about 10 percent of which—or about 150,000—form mushrooms. We've identified approximately 14,000 species to date, which means that over 90 percent of mushroom-forming fungi have not yet been identified. This is really important because knowing that 90 percent of the species out there have not yet been identified, meaning that our knowledge is exceeded by our ignorance by at least one order of magnitude, if not more, and knowing, as we now do, that these species are so essential for ecological health, it becomes ever more frightening to consider the analogy that losing these species is like losing rivets in an airplane: at what point will we approach catastrophic failure, where the ecosystem will unravel? We already know, to provide just one example, that flying squirrels and voles are dependent upon truffles, and we know that in old growth forests the main predators of flying squirrels and voles are spotted owls. This means that killing off truffles kills off flying squirrels and voles, which kills off spotted owls.

That's one food chain. While there are many of these we can identify, there are many we cannot. Remember, our ignorance of the identity of the species themselves—much less the relationships between them—exceeds our knowledge by at least an order of magnitude. That problem is compounded by the fact that biological systems are inherently so complex that their complexity far exceeds our cognitive tools.

DJ: It's like David Ehrenfeld said, that not only is nature more complex than we think, it's more complex than we can think.

PS: This is especially true when we try to understand biological systems using some sort of linear logic. Any discussion about our understanding of the natural world should really start by acknowledging that we are essentially children when it comes to this.

DJ: Let's go back in time. In your book you say that animals are more closely related to fungi than to any other kingdom. I had no idea.

PS: Yes. In many ways we have far more in common with fungi than we do with plants. We respire carbon dioxide, so do fungi. We inhale oxygen, so do fungi. One of the big differences is that animals have their stomachs on the inside.

DJ: I don't understand.

PS: About 600 million years ago we diverged from fungi. The branch of fungi leading to animals evolved to capture nutrients by surrounding their food with cellular sacs, essentially primitive stomachs. As species emerged from aquatic habitats, organisms adapted means to prevent moisture loss. In terrestrial creatures, skin composed of many layers of cells emerged as a barrier against infection. Taking a different evolutionary path, the mycelium retained its netlike form of interweaving chains of cells and went underground, forming a vast food web upon which life flourished.

DJ: So in a sense mycelium kept their stomach on the outside, growing to where the food was, and animals developed internal stomachs and traveled there.

PS: But let's go even farther back. Fungi were the first organisms on land, about 1.3 billion years ago. Fungi prepared the way for everyone else. They munched rocks. They mineralized rocks. They produced enzymes and acids that pulled calcium, magnesium, iron, and all sorts of other minerals directly from rocks through their mycelium. They converted these rocks into usable foods for others. Plants followed 600 million years later.

Evolution on this planet has been largely steered, in terms of fungi, by at least two cataclysmic events. One of these was an asteroid impact (or more likely, massive and repeated volcanic eruptions) 250 million years ago, which caused massive devastation. We know from the fossil record that over 90 percent of the species disappeared and the earth became shrouded in dust. Sunlight was cut off. In the darkness, of course, massive plant communities died. And fungi inherited the earth. Organisms that paired with fungi through natural selection were rewarded. Then light came back after the skies cleared and evolution went on its course toward mass speciation. Sixty-five million years ago, bam! It happened again. We were hit by an asteroid. Massive debris was jettisoned into the atmosphere, the earth became shrouded in dust, darkness ensued for decades. Another massive die-off; that's when the dinosaurs died. Organisms that paired with fungi were re-rewarded by natural selection and fungi reinherited the earth. The point is that these asteroid impacts steered symbiosis with fungi, and fungi have been very eloquent in their choosing of symbiotic partners.

DJ: I don't understand.

PS: It's not just animals who are symbiotic with fungi. It's bacteria. It's viruses. All sorts of organisms have paired up with fungi. Fungi are fundamental to life on this planet. They are ancient, they are widespread, and they form partnerships with many other species.

DJ: Can you give me some examples?

PS: Yes. Fungi in the genus *Curvularia* are endophytic, meaning they grow in the stems and leaves of plants. The *Curvularia* fungi are ascomycetes, which means they're related to ergot fungi, which include *Claviceps*. The story of these fungi has several threads. One of these threads is that Meso-American ranchers realized that when their horses eat a certain type of grass, which the ranchers call "sleepy grass"—the horses basically get stoned. It takes several days for the effects of this grass to wear off to where the ranchers can move their horses again. When scientists studied "sleepy grass," they found that it wasn't the grass that was causing the horses to get stoned, but an endophytic fungus.

Another thread starts at Yellowstone Hot Springs and at Lassen Volcanic Park and elsewhere, where people noticed that some grasses can survive in extremely high temperatures—up to 160°F, in direct contact with scalding hot water. Scientists cultured some of these grasses in a laboratory, and they saw they contained a fungus. At first they thought, "Oh, it's a contaminant." So they separated this fungus from the grass cells and tried to regrow the grass. But without the fungus the grass died at around 110°. So they reintroduced this fungus and grew the grass and fungus as a symbiotic culture, and once again the grass survived to 160°, because the *Curvularia* fungus confers thermo-tolerance to the grass. That got these scientists excited at the idea of perhaps getting this *Curvularia* to convey heat tolerance to corn, rice, and wheat so that these grasses could be grown under drought conditions or in extremely arid environments.

Here's another thread. Researchers published a paper about a possible relationship between *Curvularia* and tomato plants. A different group of researchers got a *Curvularia* fungus from cold storage at a culture bank and joined it with tomatoes, expecting that it would confer thermo-tolerance. But the tomatoes all died at 105°. Why was that? They finally discovered that wild *Curvularia* fungus also carries within it a virus, and the cold storage had killed the virus. When they reintroduced the virus back into the *Curvularia* cultures and then reassociated it to tomato plants, the plants survived the heat. The plants selected the fungus, the fungus selected the virus, and the three of them, joining together, could survive extreme conditions.

These stories are just the tip of the iceberg when it comes to the intelligence of nature, and how these different entities choose partners to the benefit of all.

DJ: Of course this raises the question of who we are. Is that tomato the fungus, is it the virus? Where do our boundaries start and stop? Who are you?

PS: We're not just one organism. We are composites. Every species out there has a label that we've put on it to create a language so we can communicate the identities of what we see as the phenotypes in nature. So we can look at a tree and say it's a Douglas fir and look at an animal and say it's a harbor seal. But, indeed, when I speak to you, Derrick, I am a composite of microbes that are unified with one voice. And so I guess you could say I am the elected voice of a microbial community. This is the way of life on our planet. It is based on these complex symbiotic relationships.

When we originally split from fungi, we went the overland route and fungi went the underground route. Mycelial mats can be thousands of acres. The largest organism in the world is a mycelial mat in eastern Oregon that's 2,200 acres and more than two thousand years old. It's one cell wall thick. How is it that this vast mycelial network can be surrounded by hundreds of millions of microbes per gram trying to eat the mycelium, which is highly nutritious, and yet the cellular network is protected by one cell wall? We have five or six skin layers to protect us from infection; the mycelium has one. It protects itself by being in constant biochemical communication with its ecosystem.

These mycelial mats are neuromicrological networks. They evolved using means we don't understand but which can be demonstrated. The mycelium produces enzymes and acids externally, digests its nutrients external to its networks, and then brings in the compounds it needs for nutrition. It inhales oxygen and exhales carbon dioxide, just like we do.

They are also sentient. They know when you are there. As you walk through a forest and you break twigs underneath your feet, the mycelium surges upwards to try to capture those newly available nutrients as quickly as possible. The mats produce pharmacological compounds that activate receptor sites in our neurons and serotonin-like compounds including psilocybin. They would only activate those receptor sites if there was some evolutionary common denominator between the two, and this speaks to the fact that we evolved from fungi.

Nature is built upon its prior successes, and through natural selection. These networks are extremely resilient and adaptive to catastrophia. If you go up to disturb a mycelial network, it will say "thank you" and just regrow.

I have long spoken to the existence of fungal intelligence. I have proposed that mycelium is the earth's natural internet, and I have gotten some flak for this. But recently Nick Reed and another group of scientists in Oxford and in Edinburgh published several papers talking about the architecture of mycelium and how it's organized. They focused on the nodes of crossing, which are the branches the mycelium makes and the inter-branchings which allow the mycelium, if there is a breakage or an infection, to choose an alternative route so it can grow. There's not one specific point on the network that can shut it down. Well, the nodes of crossing organized by the mycelium conforms to the same mathematical optimization curves that internet theorists and scientists have developed to optimize the computer internet. Or rather, I guess I should say that the internet conforms to the same optimization curves as the mycelium, since the mycelium came first. Nature has already optimized its networks as we struggle to optimize our computer networks.

DJ: And then there's the question of the slime mold in the maze.

PS: Absolutely. A number of Japanese researchers put a slime mold in a maze with five exits. Three of the exits were dead ends, and two had oat rewards the slime mold could eat. The slime mold navigated the maze, found the oats. Now here's where it gets interesting. When the slime mold was later reintroduced to the same maze, rather than exploring every possible route, it navigated directly to the two end points that had the oats, showing, according to the scientists, cellular intelligence.

Further, fungi are very smart at being able to adapt to a surrounding environment, and they send out messenger molecules—which we know extremely little about, by the way—that anticipate in advance of contact the very nutrient profiles they're going to soon encounter.

Over the years I've had a lot of arguments with people about the intelligence of fungi. For a long time my brother Bill challenged me, "How can you say fungi are intelligent, and how can you say nature is intelligent?" I tried various arguments with him, and as nearly always happens on this subject, it comes down to how we define intelligence.

DJ: I've always thought a good marker of intelligence would be not destroying the planet you live on.

PS: That would certainly be one measure.

I think that any discussion of cross-species measures of intelligence is unfair anyway, because we're using the wrong language and the wrong lexicons to begin with. Won't the intelligence of mycelium be different, and be measured differently, than our own? Wouldn't the same be true for other species? All that said, none of my arguments succeeded in convincing my brother until I said, "Let's try this. You agree we are born of nature, right? Can you see the hypocrisy of you, with your brain that nature has given you, articulating the thought that nature might not be intelligent?"

Finally he conceded.

If we are born of nature, and if we are intelligent, how can you possibly think other than that nature is intelligent?

Unfortunately, I think intellectually a lot of humans have their heads in the sand. There are others who are looking around, and we are slowly developing the language tools to talk about the deep intelligence of nature. But we're moving slowly, so slowly, and I think our descendants . . .

DJ: Presuming humans survive . . .

PS: . . . will look back at us as people who unfortunately had the power to devastate ecosystems but failed to have the wisdom to not do so.

And this imbalance puts everybody at jeopardy. It's estimated that 50 percent of the species known on this planet will become extinct in the next hundred years. That means that we are entering into the sixth great known extinction on this planet, and the first one caused by humans. The ramifications of this are unraveling the very network that has given rise to life. As we undermine those networks, we are harming our descendents' future and may imperil our own species' survival.

People making significant decisions in this culture do so on the basis of increasing short-term profits. That short-sightedness ultimately imperils their own children.

DJ: It imperils everyone's children, human and nonhuman alike.

PS: We have responsibilities to leave the planet in a healthier state than that which we inherited.

DJ: You think?

PS: Yeah. Who knew?

DJ: So now, at last, to how mycelium can help save the world. Can we talk for a moment about mycoremediation? I'm thinking of oyster mushrooms.

PS: And oil. Yes.

Oil, as you know, originally came from decomposing plant matter. And the same bonds that hold wood and other plant material together also hold oil together. So the enzymes these forest fungi produce are exquisitely well designed to break down substances with hydrogen-carbon bonds, which include most petroleum products, most petroleum-based pesticides, and many other toxic compounds—benzenes, dioxins, and so on—that are destroying so much of the natural world (and our own bodies).

In the specific case of oyster mushrooms and oil, for more than thirty years the Washington State Department of Transportation (WSDOT) operated a maintenance yard for trucks. Diesel and oil contaminated the soil at levels approaching 2 percent, or twenty thousand parts per million, about the same concentration found on the beaches of Prince William Sound after the Exxon Valdez spill. In 1998 I was involved in an experiment in which the WSDOT set aside four piles of contaminated soil. Each pile was about three to four feet high, eight feet wide, and about twenty feet long. One pile was left untreated, one pile was inoculated with bacteria, one was treated with chemical enzymes, and the fourth was treated with oyster mushroom spawn. The piles were covered. Four weeks later the covers were removed. The first three were black and stank like diesel fuel and oil. The fourth, the one inoculated with mushroom spawn, had a huge flush of hundreds of mushrooms growing from it, some up to a foot across. The pile no longer stank. Five weeks later, plants began to grow on the previously polluted pile. In the meantime, the mushrooms had attracted insects who laid their eggs in the fruits. These eggs hatched, and the larvae attracted birds, who pooped out seeds and introduced even more plants. Other mushrooms also began to appear. In less than eight weeks the total petroleum hydrocarbons went from twenty thousand parts per million down to two hundred parts per million. Further, even among the toxins which remained, the mushrooms had converted the larger, more toxic molecules into smaller, less toxic molecules. And finally, one of the WSDOT employees who loved mushrooms wanted to take the oysters home and eat them. We discouraged that, since we didn't know what contaminants they might not have metabolized, but subsequent analysis revealed that the mushrooms contained no detectable amounts of petroleum residues (we didn't check for heavy metals). The primary by-products were mushrooms, carbon dioxide, and water.

DJ: It was, as you say, a mycomiracle.

PS: Life was flowering on what had been a dead landscape.

Here's another example. I provided Battelle Laboratories with twenty-six strains of my fungi for screening. One day I received a report marked confidential and classified, but I saw that I was named as a coauthor. The report was on the destruction of chemical warfare components. I called up my associates, and they said, "We tested your strain library against some very potent neurotoxins, which the U.S. government is quite concerned about, including Sarin, Somin, and VX, which Saddam Hussein used against the Kurds. Two of your strains did very well breaking down VX and so we pursued this . . ."

And this is the really interesting part, which I think speaks to how adaptive these fungi are. The person I was talking to said they took these two strains and serially transferred them from one culture plate to another, then another, then another, and so on. Every time they transferred them, they increased the amount of the VX components called DMMP—dimethyl methylphosphonate, which is the core toxic constituent of nerve gas—and decreased the amount of other nutrients—malt sugar, yeast, peptone, and things like that. At the end of the experiment, the sole nutrient source was DMMP, this nerve gas agent. There were no other nutrients in the dish, and the cultures grew luxuriantly. So the fungus was able to adapt its enzyme suites specifically to the available nutrition. This is one way they govern ecosystems. They are extremely adaptive.

DJ: Can mushrooms break down plastics?

PS: My understanding is that bacteria do a better job first, and then the mycelium comes second. But there are two million species of fungi, so there are a lot of candidates that can adapt and break down resources, including plastic.

DJ: Instead of throwing away all this PVC or Styrofoam, would it be feasible to have mushrooms eat them? I guess there are two ways to put this question. One is, what sort of remediation can we do? The other is, if humans disappeared tomorrow, what would eventually happen to all the styrofoam? Would fungi presumably figure out a way to eat it?

PS: I would never underestimate the power of fungi. They are the grand molecular disassemblers in nature. And this is what they do: they unravel complex compounds into smaller edible compounds. Challenging fungi or having enough microdiversity in the ecosphere will enable those best candidates to surge forward and take advantage of that resource.

It may take time, and it may not happen in our lifetimes, but it will happen. Relative to geologic time, I think these fungi will do quite a good job of returning nutrients back into the carbon bank.

DJ: Given these mycomiracles, why don't they have fungi emergency response teams that can rush out and drop fungi onto oil spills or other contaminated places?

PS: In my book I list a number of patents, some of which are blocking patents. Some of these blocking patents expire this year.

DJ: Blocking patents?

PS: I was working with a company called Battelle to industrialize this technology, and Battelle received a nasty letter from a lawyer representing a patent holder who wanted to block us. He had no experience growing mycelium outdoors or other than inside of a petri dish, but he had been able to get a patent almost seventeen years before.

Luckily, seventeen years is classically the duration or lifetime of patents. With these blocking patents expiring, a lot of this information will soon be in the public domain. And there's a huge surge in interest in mycoremediation. I'm being peppered almost on a daily basis with different projects and requests. In Mason County, Washington, where I live, the shellfish industry is being threatened from contamination from upland owners, and I am involved in several projects to ameliorate the impact of these pollutants. That's really what *Mycelium Running* is all about: it's a manual for the mycological rescue of the planet.

DJ: Oil, VX . . .

PS: Here's another example. The BioShield program of the U.S. Defense Department and I signed contracts about four or five years ago searching for fungi that will help in the fight against bioterrorism. Bioterrorism is very scary. You can track nuclear weapons because of their radioactive signature, but you can't track viruses in the same way, so they are much more of a stealth terrorist weapon.

Old growth forests are habitat for a mushroom called *Fomitopsis officinalis*, otherwise known as agarikon, now thought to be largely extinct in Europe because it's exclusive to old growth forest habitats; without old growth forests this mushroom doesn't grow. We still have it in Washington, Oregon, British Columbia, and Northern California. I sent the Defense Department a few hundred agarikon extracts, and the BioShield program began testing them. Well, we have extremely credible evidence that this particular mushroom produces antismallpox compounds. Those of us born after 1980 have not been immunized against smallpox. Al Qaeda is believed to have bought smallpox virus from the disintegrating republics in Russia. An epidemic today would cause mass devastation, because we have no antidote. If it ramped across the landscape, 30 percent of us would be killed within two weeks, 30 percent of us would be horribly scarred and maimed—pox cavities all over our faces and arms—30 percent of us would become blind, and around 10 percent of us would survive with no physical scars. This mushroom, if it indeed proves to be effective against smallpox as a treatment for humans—prevention or after the fact—could literally save millions of lives. And so I think we can make the argument that we should save old growth forests as a matter of national defense. Biodiverse areas hold many other treasures that we will need to depend upon in time. The loss of these niche environments will be extremely detrimental to our future.

Yet another example. The hideous *Gomphidius glutinosus* is a slimy mychorhizal mushroom that grows all over the conifer forests of the world. It is a hyper-accumulator of caesium-137, a radioactive substance that Chernobyl spewed into the atmosphere. The Ukrainians were quite concerned about locals eating mushrooms, so they analyzed different mushrooms for their radioactivity and their heavy metals. Lo and behold, this one mushroom concentrates caesium-137 more than ten thousand times the background contamination, making it highly radioactive. Why would nature do that? The mushroom became hot, radioactively speaking, but the surrounding ecosystem lost its radioactivity. The fungi had a governing, mothering influence on the ecosystem, detoxifying it for the benefit of the community. By removing the fungi it could be possible to detoxify that ecosystem, at least marginally so.

DJ: Are you saying what I think you're saying?

PS: I'm saying that mushrooms are very clever at surveying a landscape and taking a long-term view of the health of the population of the descendent organisms that give rise to the forest, that create the debris fields, that feed the fungi, that help the fungi's own progeny live downstream. They take a very advanced view of ecosystem health and management, trying to increase soil depth and richness, thus increasing the carrying capacity of the ecosystem. Higher carrying capacity leads to more biodiversity, more sustainability, more resiliency. Soil is also a great carbon bank. A good way of sequestering carbon dioxide out of the atmosphere is embedding it in soil, and in doing so we all benefit.

DJ: Mothering. Governing. The mushrooms are tending to the health of the forest.

PS: Here's another example. Two excellent authors, Simard and Arndebrandt, were curious about how trees survive in the shade of thick forests. How do they get enough food?

If you've been in an old growth forest, you've probably seen hemlock trees on rotting nurse logs. They're usually the first trees to come up in highly shaded environments. They have very little exposure to light. When these small saplings were dug up and taken to a greenhouse-like environment and given a similar amount of low light, they all died. The question became, where are these young trees getting their nutrients? So the researchers radioactively tagged carbon molecules and watched their translocation. They found that birch and alder trees growing in more riparian habitats—along rivers—where there is more sunlight, were contributing nutrients to the hemlocks via mycelium.

DJ: Wait. Are they . . .

PS: Yes. The mycelium—which if you remember run all through the forest soil and connect different parts of the forest to each other like some form of internet—transfer nutrients from trees of one species who have nutrients to spare to trees of another species who need nutrients or they will die. The mycelium take care of the health of the forest. I think these fungi have come to learn through evolution that biodiversity and the resiliency of ecosystems benefit all the members of the forest, not just one.

DJ: I think the sentence I loved most from your entire book was, "Nature loves a community." If every person in the world understood that, this culture wouldn't be killing the planet.

PS: I agree.

My mother is a charismatic Christian. I grew up in a highly charismatic Christian environment between the ages of ten to seventeen, before I left Ohio. My mother's a wonderful lady. She's very kind and generous. She's the most wonderful mother in the world, in my opinion. I love her deeply. And she raised five children, all of whom are very scientifically oriented. This makes for an interesting contrast between different belief systems. No, my mother doesn't believe that the earth started six thousand years ago, but we have interesting dialogues. It seems that sometimes she feels a little nervous because most of her friends have viewpoints that are sort of antiscientific. So one day I had this epiphany just as I was waking up, and I called her and said, "I think I have a bridge of understanding that can unify the creationists with the evolutionists."

She's always very interested in what I'm thinking. She said, "Well, what is it?" I said, "Evolution is God's intelligent design."

She liked it. She and I agree on several things. We agree that when it comes to God and nature, our understanding is incomplete. No one can claim that they truly know God, and if they did, they would be an egomaniac. Similarly, no one can claim they truly understand nature, and if they did, they, too, would be an egomaniac.

Knowing that our knowledge and view of nature and/or God is inadequate to a task, we can, once again, recognize that the complexity of the universe exceeds our ability to understand it. Now, whether nature is God—which is my bet right now—may be open to interpretation, but I think there is a lot of more common ground between so-called creationists and so-called evolutionists than we normally think.

DJ: Terence McKenna, who is known for, among other things, his work with psilocybin, said of the mushroom, "I am old, older than thought in your species, which is itself fifty times older than your history."

PS: Psilocybin is a neurotransmitter that temporarily substitutes for serotonin. The neurological networks in our brain utilize these dimethyl tryptamines which are also being utilized by the mushroom mycelium. These fungi are producing the very same classes of neurotransmitters that enable us to think.

Stop and consider the ramifications of this.

DJ: And you've worked with psilocybin.

PS: My work with psilocybin goes back a long ways. I was covered for more than twenty years by a DEA permit. I've published five new species, four of which are psilocybin-active mushrooms, in the scientific literature.

My experience with ingesting these mushrooms has definitely been very spiritual and very important to me. There is a common theme that I experience every time I ingest them. I hear voices from nature screaming out to me, saying, "Don't you see? Don't you know? Please wake up!" They say, "The earth is in peril. We need your help. You're harming the earth."

This sort of global consciousness of nature infuses my experience. And I realize that I am not apart from nature. I am part of nature. And these experiences have really been my call to arms, so to speak, my call to mycological arms, to pick up the mycelial torch and march forward with it.

But I'm also pragmatic and practical. I like to see things get done. A lot of people talk a lot and don't walk their talk. Anyone around me knows I'm a workaholic. My phrase is "Walk and talk if you want to talk to me, because I'm busy." The inspiration to work this hard came from my psilocybin experiences, and now my life-long mission and goal and responsibility is to make people aware that nature is threatened, and to help them understand that by enhancing these mycelial networks, we can support and encourage nature.

Mycelium is a way to brighter, richer horizons. It is an untapped resource. It's literally underfoot. Just go outside to any piece of wood that's been on the ground and tip it over. You'll find mycelium. It's everywhere. It's the foundation of the food web. It infuses all habitats, creating microcavities that swell with water. Some myceliated habitats are spongy habitats that hold water, helping all these other organisms to thrive. We should never forget that we have fungal allies in our ecosystem. And we should engage and use mycelium. Ally ourselves with them. They are a powerful ally calling out to us.

DJ: What are some tangible things that people can do to support the mycelial networks in their community?

PS: Buy a mushroom kit. Teach your children. I became a biologist the day in kindergarten when I planted a sunflower seed in my little Dixie cup. That seed germinated and the first leaves stretched toward the sun—I felt so alive. Seeing the genesis of life is an important experience that all children should have at the earliest possible age. I once went to a highbrow conference with all these great speakers and scientists and really advanced computer mathematical geniuses. I'll never forget this one guy who was into the most advanced type of computer technologies. He was a great speaker and had great depth of knowledge, but I was devastated and shocked when he admitted that his five-year-old son has never handled soil.

DJ: Oh my god.

PS: Is this the way of the future?

A naturalist conducting ecological studies in China wrote me, "There are no frogs or butterflies within thirty kilometers of Shanghai." He was devastated. Most cities are committing ecological suicide. Our whole culture is committing ecological suicide. If this disease of urbanization spreads across the world, it doesn't take a rocket scientist to understand that we will pollute ourselves out of existence.

That's why I think it's important to teach children about life cycles, about biogenesis, mycogenesis, the sudden growth of organisms. We must teach these children to be good caretakers and good custodians. When you own your successes, whether it's growing a mushroom kit, caring for a sunflower, or just sitting and watching a tadpole, you're proud and happy and connected. You have discovered the value of knowing life.

MARTÍN PRECHTEL

Interview conducted at his home
in New Mexico, 2001.

Martín Prechtel was raised in New Mexico on a Pueblo Indian reservation where people still lived in the old, pre-European ways. His mother was a Canadian Indian who taught at the Pueblo school, and his father was a white paleontologist. Martín loved the culture there and the land. "I spent the whole of my very early life," he says, "in a state of weepy terror about the possibility of the total annihilation of this beautiful world at the hands of a few white men who couldn't understand the beauty we had in this way of life." He began to work against this dangerous, beauty-killing power. "The natives called it 'white man ways,'" he says, "but it was more than that. Its infectious power had eaten the whites, too, and made them its obvious promoter. This horrible syndrome had no use for the truly natural, the wild nature of all peoples."

In 1970, after his first marriage ended and his mother died, Prechtel went to Mexico to clear his head. Seemingly by accident, he ended up going into Guatemala. He traveled around that country for more than a year before he came to a village called Santiago Atitlán. The village was inhabited by the Tzutujil, one of many indigenous Mayan subcultures, each of which has its own distinct traditions, patterns of clothing, and language.

In Santiago Atitlán, a strange man came up to Prechtel and said, "What took you so long? For two years I've been calling you. Let's get to work!" So began his apprenticeship to Nicolas Chiviliu, one of the greatest of the Tzutujil Mayan shamans.

The apprenticeship lasted several years. As a shaman, Prechtel would learn how to correct imbalances in people's relationships with the ancestors and the spirits. He also had to learn the Tzutujil language. (Women taught him at first, and because women and men talk differently, he was a great source of amusement when he began to speak in public.)

Though not a native, Prechtel became a full member of the village. He married a local woman and had three sons, one of whom died. When Chiviliu died, Prechtel took his place, becoming shaman to nearly thirty thousand people. He also rose to the public office of Nabey Mam, or first chief. One of his duties as chief was to lead the young village men through their long initiations into adulthood.

Prechtel wanted to stay in Santiago Atitlán forever, but during the time that he lived there, Guatemala was in the throes of a civil war. The ruling government— with its U.S.-backed death squads—had outlawed the thousand-year-old Mayan rites. Ultimately, Prechtel was forced to flee for his life. "I was going to stay," he says, "but before my teacher died, he asked me to leave so that I wouldn't get killed. He wanted me to carry on the knowledge that he had passed to me."

Prechtel brought his family to the U.S., where they "just kind of starved for a while until Robert Bly and men like him found me." (Bly, a poet active in the men's movement, has high praise for Prechtel, whom he describes as "a short kind of pony that gallops through the fields of human possibility with flowers dropping out of his mouth.") Though Prechtel's wife decided to return to her native Guatemala, he remained in the U.S. with their children and currently lives not fifty miles from where he grew up.

Prechtel is the author of *Secrets of the Talking Jaguar,* in which he writes— musically, clearly, and respectfully—about the indigenous traditions in Santiago Atitlán. He gives glimpses of his training, yet never reveals details that would allow readers to steal the Mayans' spiritual traditions the way others have stolen their land. In his most recent book, *Long Life, Honey in the Heart*, Prechtel describes the structure of the village, the Tzutujil priesthood, and everyday village life before the arrival of the death squads. In addition to his writing, Prechtel paints scenes from the daily activities and mythology of the Mayan people and is a musician who has recorded several CDs.

Prechtel appears around the world at conferences on initiation for young men. ("I'm working with women on that, too," he says, "but it's a little bit slower—mostly because I'm not a woman.") He also leads workshops that help people reconnect with their own sense of place and the sacredness of ordinary life. "Spirituality is an extremely practical thing," he says. "It's not just something you choose to do on the weekends. . . . It's an everyday thing, as essential as eating or holding hands or keeping warm in the winter."

When I went to interview Prechtel at his home in New Mexico, I was embarrassed to find that my tape recorder wasn't working. Fortunately, his wife, Hanna, had a recorder I could use. It worked for about forty minutes, then started to run backward. Martín apologized, saying this sort of thing happened all the time. "I just seem to have this effect on machines," he said. "My dentist won't let me come in his front door anymore, because I freeze up all his computers." I made a note never to travel with him.

Hanna was able to coax the recorder to work again, and we finished the interview. My own tape recorder began working again the next morning, when I was about seventy miles away.

Derrick Jensen: What is a shaman?

Martín Prechtel: Shamans are sometimes considered healers or doctors, but really they are people who deal with the tears and holes we create in the net of life, the damage that we all cause in our search for survival. In a sense, all of us— even the most untechnological, spiritual, and benign peoples—are constantly wrecking the world. The question is: how do we respond to that destruction? If we respond as we do in modern culture, by ignoring the spiritual debt that we create just by living, then that debt will come back to bite us, hard. But there are other ways to respond. One is to try to repay that debt by giving gifts of beauty and praise to the sacred, to the invisible world that gives us life. Shamans deal with the problems that arise when we forget the relationship that exists between us and the other world that feeds us, or when, for whatever reason, we don't feed the other world in return.

All of this may sound strange to modern, industrialized people, but for the majority of human history, shamans have simply been a part of ordinary life. They exist all over the world. It seems strange to Westerners now because they have systematically devalued the other world and no longer deal with it as part of their everyday lives.

DJ: How are shamans from Siberia, for example, different from shamans in Guatemala?

MP: There are as many different ways to be a shaman as there are different languages, but there's a commonality, as well, because we're all standing on one earth, and there's water in the ocean wherever we go, and there's ground underneath us wherever we go. So we all have, on some level, a commonality of experience. We are all still human beings. Some of us have buried our humanity deep inside, or medicated or anesthetized it, but every person alive today, tribal or modern, primal or domesticated, has a soul that is original, natural, and, above all, indigenous in one way or another. The indigenous soul of the modern person, though, has either been banished to the far reaches of the dream world or is under direct attack by the modern mind. The more you consciously remember your indigenous soul, the more you physically remember it.

Shamans are all trying to put right the effects of normal human stupidity and repair relationships with the invisible sources of life. In many instances, the ways in which they go about this are similar. For example, the Siberians have a trance method of entering the other world that is similar to one used in Africa.

DJ: You've mentioned "the other world" a few times. Most modern people would not consciously acknowledge such a place. What is the other world?

MP: If this world were a tree, then the other world would be the roots—the part of the plant we can't see, but that puts the sap into the tree's veins. The other world feeds this tangible world—the world that can feel pain, that can eat and drink, that can fail; the world that goes around in cycles; the world where we die. The other world is what makes this world work. And the way we help the other world continue is by feeding it with our beauty.

All human beings come from the other world, but we forget it a few months after we're born. This amnesia occurs because we are dazzled by the beauty and physicality of this world. We spend the rest of our lives putting back together our memories of the other world, enough to serve the greater good and to teach the new amnesiacs—the children—how to remember. Often, this lesson is taught during the initiation into adulthood.

The Mayans say that the other world sings us into being. We are its song. We're made of sound, and as the sound passes through the sieve between this world and the other world, it takes the shape of birds, grass, tables—all these things are made of sound. Human beings, with our own sounds, can feed the other world in return, to fatten those in the other world up, so they can continue to sing.

DJ: Who are "they"?

MP: All those beings who sing us alive. You could translate it as gods or as spirits. The Mayans simply call them "they."

DJ: There's an old Aztec saying I read years ago: "That we come to this earth to live is untrue. We come to sleep and to dream." I wonder if you can help me understand it.

MP: When you dream, you remember the other world, just as you did when you were a newborn baby. When you're awake, you're part of the dream of the other world. In the "waking" state, you are supposed to dedicate a certain amount of time to feeding the world you've come from. Similarly, when you die and leave this world and go on to the next, you're supposed to feed this present dream with what you do in that one.

Dreaming is not about healing the person who's sleeping. It's about the person feeding the whole, remembering the other world, so that it can continue. The New Age falls pretty flat with the Mayans, because, to them, self-discovery is good only if it helps you to feed the whole.

DJ: Where does the Mayan concept of debt fit in?

MP: As Christians are born with original sin, Mayans are born with original debt. In the Mayan worldview, we are all born owing a spiritual debt to the other world for having created us, for having sung us into existence. It must be fed; otherwise, it's going to take its payment out of our lives.

DJ: How does one repay this debt?

MP: You have to give a gift to that which gives you life. It's an actual payment in kind. That's the spiritual economy of a village.

It's like my old teacher used to say: "You sit singing on a little rock in the middle of a pond, and your song makes a ripple that goes out to the shores where the spirits live. When it hits the shore, it sends an echo back toward you. That echo is the spiritual nutrition." When you send out a gift, you send it out in all directions at once. And then it comes back to you from all directions.

DJ: It must end up being a complex pattern, because as you're sending your song out, your neighbors are also sending theirs out, and you've got all these overlapping ripples.

MP: It's an entangled net so enormous the mind cannot possibly comprehend it. No one knows what's connected to where.

DJ: How does this relate to technology?

MP: Technological inventions take from the earth but give nothing in return. Look at automobiles. They were, in a sense, dreamed up over a period of time, with different people adding on to each other's dreams—or, if you prefer, adding on to each other's studies and trials. But all along the way, very little, if anything, was given back to the hungry, invisible divinity that gave people the ability to invent those cars. Now, in a healthy culture, that's where the shamans would come in, because with every invention comes a spiritual debt that must be paid, either ritually, or else taken out of us in warfare, grief, or depression.

A knife, for instance, is a very minimal, almost primitive tool to people in a modern industrial society. But for the Mayan people, the spiritual debt that must be paid for the creation of such a tool is great. To start with, the person who is going to make the knife has to build a fire hot enough to produce coals. To pay for that, he's got to give a sacrificial gift to the fuel, to the fire.

DJ: Like what?

MP: Ideally, the gift should be something made by hand, which is the one thing humans have that spirits don't.

Once the fire is hot enough, the knife maker must smelt the iron ore out of the rock. The part that's left over, which gets thrown away in Western culture, is the most holy part in shamanic rituals. What's left over represents the debt, the hollowness that's been carved out of the universe by human ingenuity, and so must be refilled with human ingenuity. A ritual gift equal to the amount that was removed from the other world has to be put back to make up for the wound caused to the divine. Human ingenuity is a wonderful thing, but only so long as it's used to feed the deities that give us the ability to perform such extravagant feats in the first place.

So, just to get the iron, the shaman has to pay for the ore, the fire, the wind, and so on—not in dollars and cents, but in ritual activity equal to what's been given. Then that iron must be made into steel, and the steel has to be hammered into the shape of a knife, sharpened, and tempered, and a handle must be put on it. There is a deity to be fed for each part of the procedure. When the knife is finished, it is called the "tooth of earth." It will cut wood, meat, and plants. But if the necessary sacrifices have been ignored in the name of rationalism, literalism, and human superiority, it will cut humans instead.

All of those ritual gifts make the knife enormously "expensive," and make the process quite involved and time-consuming. The need for ritual makes some things too spiritually expensive to bother with. That's why the Mayans didn't invent space shuttles or shopping malls or backhoes. They live as they do not because it's a romantic way to live—it's not; it's enormously hard—but because it works.

Western culture believes that all material is dead, and so there is no debt incurred when human ingenuity removes something from the other world. Consequently, we end up with shopping malls and space shuttles and other examples of "advanced" technology, while the spirits who give us the ability to make those things are starving, becoming bony and thin. That's one reason anorexia is such a problem: the young are acting out this image. The universe is in a state of starvation and emotional grief because it has not been given what it needs in the form of ritual food and actual physical gifts. We think we're getting away with something by stealing from the other side, but it all leads to violence.

The Greek oracle at Delphi saw this a long time ago and said, "Woe to humans, the invention of steel."

DJ: Why does this theft lead to violence?

MP: Though capable of feeding all creation, the spirit is not an omnipotent force, as Christianity would have us believe, but a natural force of great subtlety. When its subtlety is trespassed on by the clumsiness of human greed and conceit, then both human and divine nature are violated and made into hungry, devouring things. We become food for this monster our spiritual amnesia has created. The monster is fed by wars, psychological depression, self-hate, and bad world trade practices that export misery to other places.

We inflict violence upon each other as a way to replace what we steal from nature because we've forgotten this old deal that our ancestors signed so long ago. Instead, we psychologize and objectify that relationship as a personal experience or pathology, rather than a spiritual obligation. At that point, our approach to spirituality becomes rationalist armoring, a psychology of protection for the part of us that creates the greed monster, which causes us to kill the world and each other. As individuals, we become depressed, because the beings of the other world take it out of our emotions.

DJ: How so?

MP: When we no longer maintain a relationship with the spirits, the spirits have to eat our psyches. And when the spirits are done eating our psyches, they eat our bodies. And when they're done with that, they move on to the people close to us. When you have a culture that has for centuries, or longer, ignored these relationships, depression becomes a way of life. We try to fix the depression through technology, but that's never going to work. Nor will it work to plunder other cultures, nor to kill the planet. All that is just an attempt not to be held accountable to the other world. If you're to succeed as a human being, you've got to live meaningfully, passionately, and fully, so that even your death becomes a meaningful sacrifice to the spirits, feeding them. Everybody's death was a meaningful sacrifice until people started to become "civilized" and began killing everybody else's gods in the name of monotheism. As you grow older, your life becomes more and more meaningful as a sacrifice, because you give more and more gifts to the other world, and the spirits are better fed by your speech and prayers.

DJ: How do you respond to someone who says that the notion of paying a debt to the spirit world for making a knife is just inefficient, which is why we've wiped out all those cultures? In the time your group spends making one knife, my group will make three hundred knives and cut all your throats.

MP: If you take up that strategy, then you will have to live with the ghosts of those you've murdered, which means you've got to make more and more knives, and you will become more and more depressed, all the while calling yourself "advanced" to rationalize your predicament.

DJ: What are these ghosts?

MP: Before we talk any more about ghosts, we have to talk about ancestors, because the two are related.

Often, you'll hear that you have to honor your ancestors, but I believe it's much more complex than that. Our ancestors weren't necessarily very smart. In many cases, they are the ones who left us this mess. Some of them were great, but others had huge prejudices. If these ancestors are given their due, then you don't have to live out their prejudices in your own life. But if you don't give the ancestors something, if you simply say, "I'm descended from these people, but they don't affect me very much; I'm a unique individual," then you're cursed to spend your life either fighting your ancestors, or else riding the wave they started. You'll have to do that long before you can be yourself and pursue what you believe is worth pursuing.

The Mayan way of dealing with this is to give the ancestors a place to live. You actually build houses for them—called "sleeping houses"—and put your ancestors in there. The houses are small, because the ancestors don't take up any space, but they do need a designated place, just like anything else. Then you feed your ancestors with words and eloquence. We all have old, forgotten languages that our languages are descended from, and many of these languages are a great deal more ornate. But even with our current language, we still have the capacity to create strange, mysterious, poetic gifts to feed the ancestors, so that we won't become depressed by their ghosts devouring our everyday lives.

If we can get past the prejudices of the last ten thousand years' worth of ancestors, then we can find our way back to our indigenous souls and culture, where we are always at home and welcome.

DJ: My ancestry is Danish, French, and Scottish, but I live in Northern California, so how can I find my way back?

MP: The problem is not that your ancestors migrated to North America but that, when they died, their debts were not properly paid with beauty, grief, and language. Whenever someone dies, that person's spirit has to go on to the next world. If that person has not gone through an initiation and remembered where she came from and what she must do to go on, then she won't know where to go. Also, when a person dies, her spirit must return what has been taken out to feed her existence while she was on earth. All of the old burial rituals are about paying back the debt to the other world and helping the spirit to move on.

One of the ways those who remain behind can help repay this spiritual debt is simply by missing the dead. Let's say your beloved grandmother dies. Some might say you shouldn't weep, because she's going to "a better place," and weeping is just pure selfishness. But people's longing for each other and for the terrain of home is so enormous that, if you do not weep to express it, you're poisoning the future with violence. If that longing is not expressed as a loud, beautiful wail, a song, or a piece of art that's given as a gift to the spirits, then it will turn into violence against other beings—and, more importantly, against the earth itself, because you will have no understanding of home. But if you are able to feed the other world with your grief, then you can live where your dead are buried, and they will become a part of the landscape in a way.

Many old cultures had funeral arrangements whereby the dead were annually fed by the living for as long as fifty years, with the living giving ritual payments back to the world and the earth for the debts incurred by the deceased. When that grief doesn't happen, the ancestors' ghosts begin to chase the culture.

It's difficult enough when you have only a few dead people to mourn, but what happens when there are too many dead, when there is no time to mourn them all? When you get not just one or two ghosts (which a shaman might be able to help you with), but hundreds, or thousands, or millions of ghosts, because not just your ancestors, but the beings who have been trespassed against—the women who have been raped, the animals who have been slaughtered for no reason, the ground that has been torn to shreds—have all become ghosts, too?

DJ: Are you speaking metaphorically here?

MP: No, I'm talking literally. The ghosts will actually chase you, and they always chase you toward the setting sun. That's why all the great migrations of the past several thousand years have been to the west: because people are running away from the ghosts. The people stop and try to live in a new place for a while, but the ghosts always catch up with them and create enormous wars and pain and problems, which feed the hungry hordes of ghosts. Then the people continue on, always moving, never truly at home. Now we have an entire culture based on our fleeing or being devoured by ghosts.

DJ: What can we do about the ghosts?

MP: On a finite planet, we can't outrun them. We've tried to develop technology that will keep us safe: medicines to numb our grief, fortresses to keep the ghosts away. But none of it will work.

In a village, if a family is beset by a ghost, the shaman will capture the ghost, break it down into its component parts, and send them back to the other world one at a time. Then the shaman and the family will set up a regular maintenance program, to get back on track in their relationship with the other world. This is the maintenance way of living.

I'm not sure how Western culture could do this. How can members of a culture that considers the earth a dead thing possibly repay all that debt? How can they possibly get away from all those ghosts? With everything that has gone on for so long, can they ever really be at home again?

To be at home in a place, to live in a place well, we first have to understand where we are; we've got to look at our surroundings. Second, we've got to know our own histories. Third, we've got to feed our ancestors' ghosts, so that the ghosts aren't eating us or the people around us. Lastly, we've got to begin to grieve. Now, grief doesn't mean sitting around weeping every day. Rather, grief means using the gifts you've been given by the spirits to make beauty. Grief that's not expressed this way becomes a kind of toxic waste inside a person's body, and inside the culture as a whole, until it has to be put in containers and shipped someplace, the way they ship radioactive waste to New Mexico.

This locked-up grief has to be metabolized. As a culture and as individuals, we must begin feeling our grief—that delicious, fantastic, eloquent medicine. Then we can start giving spiritual gifts to the land we live on, which might someday grant our grandchildren permission to live there.

DJ: What's the relationship between grief and belonging to a place?

MP: In the Guatemalan village where I lived, you don't belong someplace until your people have died there and the living have wept for them there. Until a few of your generations have died on the land and been buried there, and your soul has fed on the land, you're still a tourist, a visitor.

While I lived in this village, one of my sons, a baby, died of typhoid. When I lost a child, I mysteriously and suddenly became a true, welcomed resident of the land. It wasn't as if I owned the land, but I was an honorable renter who'd paid with grief, artistically expressed in ritual. My child had merged with the land, so now I was related to the rocks and the trees and the air in a bodily way that I hadn't been before. And since the other villagers were all related to these same rocks and trees and air, that made us all relatives.

Now, you might say that all your ancestors from Denmark, France, and Scotland have been put in the ground in North America, so why aren't you welcome here? Why aren't you related to the rocks and the trees and the air?

It's because your ancestors who died are most likely still ghosts, still uninitiated souls who have not yet become true ancestors, because their debts were not paid with grief and beauty. Once they become true ancestors, you merge with the region, and you begin to help this world live. At that point, you'll find that you have less need for toasters and machinery and computers—less need for everything. You'll finally be starting to live well.

For us to get to that stage, we have to study eloquence, grief, and sacrifice. I'm not just talking about the type of sacrifice where somebody takes three days off to work in the neighborhood, although that may be part of it. I'm talking about giving to the nonhuman, as well as to the human.

DJ: So you're saying that we need to deal with the ghosts, and once we've dealt with them . . .

MP: Then we have to talk about maintenance, which is far more important than corrective measures. This culture is based on fixing things, as opposed to maintaining them. But once we start to maintain instead of constantly fix, the problems that vex us will become much easier to solve. It will no longer be a matter of fixing something as we think of it today. Right now, fixing something means getting our way. It should mean asking: "What do I need to do here?"

Our culture also emphasizes individual freedom, but such freedom can be enjoyed only when there is a waiting village of open-armed, laughing elders who know compassion and grasp the complexity of the spirit world well enough to catch us, keep us grounded, and protect us from ourselves.

If the modern world is to start maintaining things, it will have to redefine itself. A new culture will have to develop, in which neither humans and their inventions nor God is at the center of the universe. What should be at the center is a hollow place, an empty place where both God and humans can sing and weep together. Maybe, together, the diverse and combined excellence of all cultures could court the tree of life back from where it's been banished by our literalist minds and dogmatic religions.

DJ: Speaking of dogmatic religions, how did the Mayan traditions survive the influx of Spanish missionaries?

MP: The Spaniards came to our village in 1524, but they couldn't get anybody to go to their church, so they demolished our old temple and used the stones to build a new church on the same site. (This was a common practice.) But the Tzutujil people are crafty. They watched as the old temple stones were used to build the new church, and they memorized where each one went. As far as the Tzutujil were concerned, this strange, square European church was just a reconfiguration of the old. (When I was learning to be a shaman, I had to memorize where all those damn stones were, because they were all holy. It was like being a novice taxi driver in London.)

The Catholic priests abandoned the village in the 1600s because of earthquakes and cholera, then came back fifty years later and found a big hole in the middle of the church. "What is that?" they said.

By then, the Indians knew the priests destroyed everything relating to the native religion, so the Indians said, "When we reenact the crucifixion of Jesus, this is the hole where we put the cross."

In truth, that hole was a hollow place that was never to be filled, because it led to another hollow place left over from the temple that had been there originally, and that place was connected to all the other layers of existence.

For four and a half centuries, the Indians kept their traditions intact in a way that the Europeans couldn't see or understand. If the Spaniards asked, "Where is your God?" the Indians would point to this empty hole. But when the American clergy came in the 1950s, they weren't fooled. They said, "This is paganism." And so, eventually, they filled the empty place with concrete.

I was there when that happened, in 1976. I was livid. I went to the village council and ranted and raved about how terrible it was. The old men calmly smoked their cigars and agreed. After an hour or so, when I was out of breath, they started talking about something totally unrelated. I asked, "Doesn't anybody care about this?"

"Oh, yeah," they said. "We care. But these Christians are idiots if they think they can just eradicate the conduit from this world to the next with a little mud. That's as ridiculous as you worrying about it. But if you must do something, here's a pick, shovel, and chisel. Dig it out."

So some old men and I dug out the hole. Then the Catholics filled the hole back up, and two weeks later we dug it out again. We went back and forth this way five times until, finally, somebody made a stone cover for the hole, so the Catholics could pretend it wasn't there, and we could pull the cover off whenever we wanted to use it.

That's how the spirit is now in this country. The hole, the hollow place that must be fed, is still there, but it's covered over with spiritual amnesia. We try to fill up that beautiful hollow place with drugs, television, potato chips—anything. But it can't be filled. It needs to be kept hollow.

DJ: Why is a hollow place holy?

MP: The Mayan people understand that the world did not come out of a creator's hand, but grew out of this hollow place and became a tree whose fruit was diversity. Human beings weren't on that tree, but everything that was on that original tree eventually went into human beings. You have gourd seeds in you, and raccoons, and amoebas—everything.

When the tree finally grew to maturity, flowered, and bore fruit, the fruit was made of sound, and every piece of it that dropped to the ground sprouted and gave birth to the diverse kinds of life. Then the old tree died and became humus consisting of ancient sounds, out of which all things flourish to this day. Everything we feel, touch, and taste is actually a manifestation of that original diversity, which means that the tree isn't really dead, but dismembered, and it's constantly trying to re-member itself.

Every year in my village, when it was still intact, the young men and women who were to be initiated into adulthood went down the hole into the other world to try to bring the parent tree back to life. They put the seeds of their holy sounds and their tears into that hole where the old tree used to live long ago. And the tree grew back. But the rest of the year, the village devoured the tree's diverse forms, creating an annual need for new initiates to re-member the old provider tree back to life. The initiates were able to go down into that hollow place and restore the tree to life because they knew how to be eloquent, how to grieve, and how to fight death instead of fighting and killing other beings.

DJ: When you say "fight death," do you mean they resisted or denied its inevitability?

MP: No, on the contrary, I mean they wrestled with death. In order for there to be life, there has to be a spiritual wrestling match with death; otherwise, it becomes a literal battle that can kill you.

The problem with death is that its gods are rationalists. The Mayans have thirteen goddesses and thirteen gods of death. These deities have no imagination, which is why they have to eat and kill us—to get our souls, our imagination. Once death has your soul, it is happy and stops killing for a while. But then you must go down and ask death—with all your eloquence—to please give back your soul. When death refuses, you've got to gamble with death, because death obeys only one rule: the rule of chance. And so you use gambling bones and try to beguile death with your eloquence. That's what we call "wrestling death." You can't kill death, of course. The best you can hope for in such a match is to bring death to a standoff. Then death will say, "OK, I'll tell you what. I'm going to give you back your soul if you promise to continue to feed me this eloquence on a regular basis, and to die at your appointed hour."

During initiation, when the young men and women wrestle death, what they're doing, essentially, is signing a contract that says, "I give up the idealistic notion that I should live forever." Your soul is then returned, but you must ritually render a percentage of the fruit of your art, your eloquence, and your imagination to the other world. That's the only deal you're going to get from death. If you try to strike a better bargain, you're going to end up killing a lot of people. When an entire culture tries to make a better deal, or refuses to wrestle death with eloquence, then death comes up to the surface to eat us in a literal way, with wars and depression.

DJ: Tell me more about the indigenous soul.

MP: Every individual in the world, regardless of cultural background or race, has an indigenous soul struggling to survive in an increasingly hostile environment created by that individual's mind. A modern person's body has become a battleground between the rationalist mind—which subscribes to the values of the machine age—and the native soul. This battle is the cause of a great deal of spiritual and physical illness.

Over the last several centuries, a heartless, culture-crushing mentality has enforced its so-called progress on the earth, devouring all peoples, nature, imagination, and spiritual knowledge. Like a bulldozer, it has left a flat, homogenized streak of civilization in its wake. Every human on this earth, whether from Africa, Asia, Europe, or the Americas, has ancestors whose stories, rituals, ingenuity, language, and life ways were taken away, enslaved, banned, exploited, twisted, or destroyed by this mentality. What is indigenous—in other words, natural, subtle, hard to explain, generous, gradual, and village-oriented— in each of us has been banished to the ghettos of our heart, or hidden away from view on reservations inside the spiritual landscape. We're taught to believe that our thoughts are actually the center of our life. Like the conquering, modern culture we belong to, we understand the world only with the mind, not with the indigenous soul.

And this indigenous soul is not something that can be brought back in "wild man" or "wild woman" retreats on the weekend and then dropped when you put on your business suit. It's not something you take up because it's fun or trendy. It has to be authentic, and it has to be spiritually expensive.

DJ: Let's talk for a moment about cooptation. There are two common positions on the wider use of indigenous traditions. One is that there's nothing wrong with making a sweat lodge in your backyard for weekend retreats, while continuing to be a stockbroker on weekdays.

MP: The consumer method.

DJ: The other, to which I subscribe, is that we must respect the privacy of indigenous traditions and not mine them for our own purposes.

MP: I've made a huge effort never to do that. The truth is that I never wanted to write books about Mayan traditions in the first place. On the Pueblo reservation where I grew up, it was taboo to write, because writing freezes knowledge, and also because much knowledge becomes useless when it is not kept secret and used only under sacred conditions. And often the things that are the most sacred are the most simple and ordinary. When this ordinariness is framed in subtle, time-honored ways, it becomes extraordinary and maintains its spiritual usefulness.

DJ: The traditions you write about are not your native southwestern traditions.

MP: No, but I lived in Santiago Atitlán, in Guatemala, for many years and made my life there. I was married, with children. Then, when the U.S.-backed death squads came, more than eighteen hundred villagers were killed within seven years: shot, beaten, tortured, poisoned, chopped up, starved to death in holes, beheaded, disappeared. This took place in a village where, prior to 1979, most people had never heard a gunshot. I had a price on my head and was almost killed on three different occasions in the 1980s. I returned to the U.S. and brought my family with me. My wife later went back home, taking our two sons with her, and we separated. The boys soon returned to live with me and are now grown men.

Then, in 1992, there was another massacre, and I had to go back to Guatemala. Some young Tzutujil men met me in a pickup truck, which was strange in itself: before, nobody had owned an automobile. They put me in the back with a bunch of squash, under a tarp. Whenever we came to an army roadblock, the soldiers saw just the squash and let us pass. They didn't look very hard. (Most of the soldiers really don't want to kill anybody: they have to be goaded into it. But they do kill.)

When we'd gotten past all the roadblocks, I got to sit up front. The other passengers were all kids. This was only eight years after I'd left, and already they had forgotten the name of my teacher, who had been one of the greatest and most famous shamans around.

As we drove, they'd ask, "Do you know the story of that mountain over there?"

"Yeah," I'd say, "that's called S'kuut. It was originally in the ocean and was brought up on land by the old goddess of the reptiles."

"Who's she?"

Pretty soon the truck was going about three miles an hour because they were rediscovering, through their ancestors' ancient stories, every mountain, ravine, and boulder along our route. After about two hours, I asked, "How come you don't know any of this?"

"Well," said one, "these two are Christians, so they're not allowed to know, and the rest of us don't have parents. They were killed in the 1980s."

So there I was, this blond half-breed from the U.S.—not even any blood relation to these kids—telling them their own people's stories. I realized then that these children, as well as my own two sons, would never know the richness of village life. They were losing their connection to this place. I had to write down what I knew, but I couldn't write down the specifics—that we went to the lake and did this and put this offering there—because then those rituals could be expropriated.

My decision to leave out the details of the rituals has irritated many people in the U.S. They insist I tell them "how to do it." I always respond, "It's not technology."

DJ: You've said explicitly that the power of shamanism is not in specific words or prayers.

MP: My teacher always said that if there is to be any hope whatsoever of living well on this earth, we have to take the ancient root and put new sap in it. That doesn't mean we need to do something new, but to do something old in a new way, which takes great courage.

I decided that if I could write these books such that the oral tradition is evident to readers, memories of their own indigenous souls might begin to arise. Of course, I tell people not to get on a plane and go to Guatemala. That would bring nothing but more heartbreak and plundering. The answer must be found in your own backyard, where you live. The only reason to explore another culture is to be able to smell the poverty in your own. Even if you go to another culture and are accepted in some way, you still have an obligation not to abandon your own culture, but to return to your homeland and try to coax its alienated indigenous traditions back into everyday life and away from tribalism, fundamentalism, and corporatized, nihilistic greed.

This is true whether we're talking about traditions or natural resources. Right now, "genetic prospectors" are going to Brazil to study plants used by indigenous peoples. Why? So they can save rich, white North Americans from diseases caused by the stupidities of their own culture. They're mining other peoples' traditions to fix, mechanically, illnesses that would be much better addressed if they stayed home and dealt with their own culture's lack of imagination and grace, grieving collectively about the inescapable reality of their mortality.

People should also be aware that many things that are touted as indigenous are not. Many of the sweat lodge ceremonies, for example, are about as Jesuit as you can get. No Indian had ever heard of the Great Spirit before the 1850s. That's all from the Jesuits.

DJ: You've said that one problem with Western culture is its use of the verb "to be."

MP: When I was a child, I spoke a Pueblo language called Keres, which doesn't have the verb "to be." It was basically a language of adjectives. One of the secrets of my ability to survive and thrive in Santiago Atitlán was that the

Tzutujil language, too, has no verb "to be." Tzutujil is a language of carrying and belonging, not a language of being. Without "to be," there's no sense that something is absolutely this or that. If two people argue, they're said to be "split," like firewood, but both sides are still of the same substance. Some of the rights and wrongs that nations have fought and died to defend or obtain are not even relevant concepts to traditional Tzutujil. This isn't because the Tzutujil are somehow too "primitive" to understand right and wrong, but because their lives aren't based on absolute states or permanence. Mayans believe nothing will last on its own. That's why their lives are oriented toward maintenance rather than creation.

"Belonging to" is as close to "being" as the Tzutujil language gets. One cannot say, "She is a mother," for instance. In Tzutujil, you can only call someone a mother by saying whose mother she is, to whom she belongs. Likewise, one cannot say, "He is a shaman." One says instead, "The way of tracking belongs to him."

In order for modern Western culture to really take hold in Santiago Atitlán, the frustrated religious, business, and political leaders first had to undermine the language. Language is the glue that holds the layers of the Mayan universe together—the eloquence of the speech, the ancestral lifeline of the mythologies. The speech of the gods used to be in our very bones. But once the Westerners forced the verb "to be" upon our young, the whole archaic Mayan world disappeared into the jaws of the modern age.

In a culture with the verb "to be," one is always concerned with identity. To determine who you are, you must also determine who you are not. In a culture based on belonging, however, you must bond with others. You are defined by where you stand and whom you stand with. The verb "to be" also reduces a language, taking away its adornment and beauty, making it more efficient. The verb "to be" is very efficient. It allows you to build things.

Rather than build things, Mayans cultivate a climate that allows for the possibility of their appearance, as for a fruit or a vine. They take care of things.

In the past, when they built big monuments, it wasn't, as in modern culture, to force the world to be a certain way, but rather to repay the world with a currency proportionate to the immense gifts the gods had given the people. Mayans don't force the world to be what they want it to be. They make friends with it; they belong to life.

DJ: You've spoken a lot today about the importance of maintenance. How does that relate to the Tzutujil practice of building flimsy houses?

MP: In the village, people used to build their houses out of traditional materials, using no iron or lumber or nails, but the houses were magnificent. Many were sewn together out of bark and fiber. Like the house of the body, the house that a person sleeps in must be very beautiful and sturdy, but not so sturdy that it won't fall apart after a while. If your house doesn't fall apart, then there will be no reason to renew it. And it is this renewability that makes something valuable. The maintenance gives it meaning.

The secret of village togetherness and happiness has always been the generosity of the people, but the key to that generosity is inefficiency and decay. Because our village huts were not built to last very long, they had to be regularly renewed. To do this, villagers came together, at least once a year, to work on somebody's hut. When your house was falling down, you invited all the folks over. The little kids ran around messing up what everybody was doing. The young women brought the water. The young men carried the stones. The older men told everybody what to do, and the older women told the older men that they weren't doing it right. Once the house was back together again, everyone ate together, praised the house, laughed, and cried. In a few days, they moved on to the next house. In this way, each family's place in the village was reestablished and remembered. This is how it always was.

Then the missionaries and the businessmen and the politicians brought in tin and lumber and sturdy houses. Now the houses last, but the relationships don't.

In some ways, crises bring communities together. Even nowadays, if there's a flood, or if somebody is going to put a highway through a neighborhood, people come together to solve the problem. Mayans don't wait for a crisis to occur; they make a crisis. Their spirituality is based on choreographed disasters—otherwise known as rituals—in which everyone has to work together to remake their clothing, or each other's houses, or the community, or the world. Everything has to be maintained because it was originally made so delicately that it eventually falls apart. It is the putting back together again, the renewing, that ultimately makes something strong. That is true of our houses, our language, our relationships.

It's a fine balance, making something that is not so flimsy that it falls apart too soon, yet not so solid that it is permanent. It requires a sort of grace. We all want to make something that's going to live beyond us, but that thing shouldn't be a house or some other physical object. It should be a village that can continue to maintain itself. That sort of constant renewal is the only permanence we should wish to attain.

ABOUT FLASHPOINT PRESS

Flashpoint Press was founded by Derrick Jensen to ignite a resistance movement. Our planet is under serious threat from industrial civilization, with its consumption of biotic communities, production of greenhouse gases and environmental toxins, and destruction of human rights and human-scale cultures around the globe. This system will not stop voluntarily, and it cannot be reformed.

Flashpoint Press believes that the Left has severely limited its strategic thinking, by insisting on education, lifestyle change, and techno-fixes as the only viable and ethical options. None of these responses can address the scale of the emergency now facing our planet. We need both a serious resistance movement and a supporting culture of resistance that can inspire and protect frontline activists. Flashpoint embraces the necessity of all levels of action, from cultural work to militant confrontation. We also intend to win.

FLASHPOINT PRESS
CRESCENT CITY, CALIFORNIA

ABOUT DERRICK JENSEN

Hailed as the philosopher poet of the ecological movement, Derrick Jensen is the widely acclaimed author of *Endgame*, *A Language Older than Words*, and *The Culture of Make Believe,* among many others. Jensen's writing has been described as "breaking and mending the reader's heart" (*Publishers Weekly*). His books with PM include: *How Shall I Live My Life?: On Liberating the Earth from Civilization* and the novels *Songs of the Dead* and *Lives Less Valuable*.

Author, teacher, activist, and leading voice of uncompromising dissent, he regularly stirs auditoriums across the country with revolutionary spirit. Jensen holds a degree in mineral engineering physics from the Colorado School of Mines, and has taught at Eastern Washington University and Pelican Bay Prison. He lives in Crescent City, California.

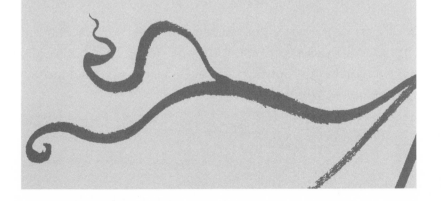

PO Box 23912
Oakland, CA 94623
www.pmpress.org

PM Press was founded at the end of 2007 by a small collection of folks with decades of publishing, media, and organizing experience. PM Press co-conspirators have published and distributed hundreds of books, pamphlets, CDs, and DVDs. Members of PM have founded enduring book fairs, spearheaded victorious tenant organizing campaigns, and worked closely with bookstores, academic conferences, and even rock bands to deliver political and challenging ideas to all walks of life. We're old enough to know what we're doing and young enough to know what's at stake.

We seek to create radical and stimulating fiction and non-fiction books, pamphlets, t-shirts, visual and audio materials to entertain, educate and inspire you. We aim to distribute these through every available channel with every available technology - whether that means you are seeing anarchist classics at our bookfair stalls; reading our latest vegan cookbook at the café; downloading geeky fiction e-books; or digging new music and timely videos from our website.

PM Press is always on the lookout for talented and skilled volunteers, artists, activists and writers to work with. If you have a great idea for a project or can contribute in some way, please get in touch.

FRIENDS OF PM PRESS

These are indisputably momentous times – the financial system is melting down globally and the Empire is stumbling. Now more than ever there is a vital need for radical ideas.

In the year since its founding – and on a mere shoestring – PM Press has risen to the formidable challenge of publishing and distributing knowledge and entertainment for the struggles ahead. With over 100 releases to date, we have published an impressive and stimulating array of literature, art, music, politics, and culture. Using every available medium, we've succeeded in connecting those hungry for ideas and information to those putting them into practice.

Friends of PM allows you to directly help impact, amplify, and revitalize the discourse and actions of radical writers, filmmakers, and artists. It provides us with a stable foundation from which we can build upon our early successes and provides a much-needed subsidy for the materials that can't necessarily pay their own way. You can help make that happen – and receive every new title automatically delivered to your door once a month – by joining as a Friend of PM Press. And, we'll throw in a free T-Shirt when you sign up.

Here are your options:

* $25 a month: Get all books and pamphlets plus 50% discount on all webstore purchases
* $25 a month: Get all CDs and DVDs plus 50% discount on all webstore purchases
* $40 a month: Get all PM Press releases plus 50% discount on all webstore purchases
* $100 a month: Superstar - Everything plus PM merchandise, free downloads, and 50% discount on all webstore purchases

For those who can't afford $25 or more a month, we're introducing Sustainer Rates at $15, $10 and $5. Sustainers get a free PM Press t-shirt and a 50% discount on all purchases from our website.

Your Visa or Mastercard will be billed once a month, until you tell us to stop. Or until our efforts succeed in bringing the revolution around. Or the financial meltdown of Capital makes plastic redundant. Whichever comes first.

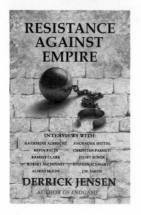
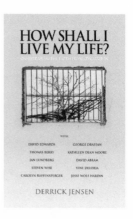

Mischief in the Forest: A Yarn Yarn (with Stephanie McMillan) $14.95

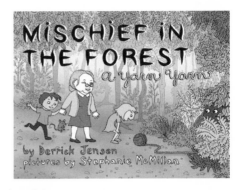

Grandma Johnson lives alone in the forest and loves to knit sweaters and mittens for her grandchildren. One day, her mischievous forest neighbors reveal themselves in a delightfully colorful fashion. This picture book inspires both young and old to connect with one's surroundings and embrace the role of good neighbors with the rest of the natural world, whether in the city or in the forest.

Lives Less Valuable
$18 (e-Book $10)

In the heart of a city, a river is dying, children have cancer, and people are burning with despair. From the safe distance that wealth buys, a corporation called Vexcorp counts these lives as another expense on a balance sheet. But that distance is about to collapse. Derrick Jensen has written a novel as compelling as it is necessary: With our planet under serious threat, Malia's decisions face us all.

Songs of the Dead
$20 (e-Book $10)

In this thriller, a serial killer stalks the streets of Spokane, acting out a misogynist script from the dark heart of this culture. Across town, a writer has spent his life tracking the reasons—political, psychological, spiritual—for the sadism of modern civilization. And through the grim nights, Nika, a trafficked woman, tries to survive the grinding violence of prostitution. Their lives, and the forces propelling them, are about to collide.

END:CIV: Resist or Die (directed and produced by Franklin Lopez) [DVD] $19.95

END:CIV examines our culture's addiction to systematic violence and environmental exploitation, and probes the resulting epidemic of poisoned landscapes and shell-shocked nations. Based in part on Derrick Jensen's bestselling book *Endgame*, *END:CIV* asks: "If your homeland was invaded by aliens who cut down the forests, poisoned the water and air, and contaminated the food supply, would you resist?" Backed by Jensen's narrative, *END:CIV* features interviews with more than 20 leading activists and thinkers.

With gratitude to the
Wallace Global Fund
for their continued support.